Aristotle

THE POETICS

Aristotle

THE POETICS

[Edited with Complete Introduction, Biography, Author's Background, Complete Text, Select Criticism and Bibliography]

Misha Kandhari
M.A., M. Phil. English,
Delhi University

ANMOL PUBLICATIONS PVT. LTD.
NEW DELHI - 110 002 (INDIA)

ANMOL PUBLICATIONS PVT. LTD.

H.O.: 4374/4B, Ansari Road, Darya Ganj,
New Delhi-110 002 (India)
Ph.: 23278000, 23261597

B.O.: No. 1015, Ist Main Road, BSK IIIrd Stage
IIIrd Phase, IIIrd Block
Bangalore - 560 085 (India)
Visit us at: www.anmolpublications.com

The Poetics

First Published, 2009

PRINTED IN INDIA

Printed at Mehra Offset Press, Delhi.

Contents

Preface

Aristotle (together with Socrates and Plato) is one of the most important founding figures in Western philosophy. He was the first to create a comprehensive system of philosophy, encompassing morality and aesthetics, logic and science, politics and metaphysics. Aristotle's views on the physical sciences profoundly shaped medieval scholarship, and their influence extended well into the Renaissance, although they were ultimately replaced by modern physics. In the biological sciences, some of his observations were only confirmed to be accurate in the nineteenth century. His works contain the earliest known formal study of logic, which were incorporated in the late nineteenth century into modern formal logic. In metaphysics, Aristotelianism had a profound influence on philosophical and theological thinking in the Islamic and Jewish traditions in the Middle Ages, and it continues to influence Christian theology, especially Eastern Orthodox theology, and the scholastic tradition of the Roman Catholic Church. All aspects of Aristotle's philosophy continue to be the object of active academic study today.

Though Aristotle wrote many elegant treatises and dialogues (Cicero described his literary style as "a river of gold"), it is thought that the majority of his writings are now lost; it is believed that only about one third of the original works have survived.

Author

Chapter 1

About Aristotle Poetics

Though the precise origins of Aristotle's *Poetics* are not known, researchers believe that the work was composed around 330 BCE and was preserved primarily through Aristotle's students' notes. Despite its vague beginning, the *Poetics* has been a central document in the study of aesthetics and literature for centuries, proving especially influential during the Renaissance; it continues to have relevance in scholarly circles today.

Over the years the *Poetics* has been both praised and disparaged. Some critics object to Aristotle's theory of poetics and regret that the work has held such sway in the history of Western literature. One contemporary critic argues that Aristotle "reduces drama to its language," and the "language itself to its least poetic element, the story, and then encourages insensitive readers...to subject stories to crudely moralistic readings that reduce tragedies to the childish proportions of Aesop-fables". Other critics have argued against such views and reclaimed the *Poetics* for their own times; often these critics emphasize the importance of reading the *Poetics* in its historical context - it was, after all, written an awfully long time ago - and stress that despite this historical barrier the insights contained in the work still hold true. Whichever side of the debate you end up on, it is important when studying the *Poetics* to take time to decode its dense text. The *Poetics* is widely considered one of Aristotle's most demanding but rewarding texts, requiring commitment in its study, but offering profound returns to the diligent reader.

The *Poetics* is Aristotle's attempt to explain the basic

problems of art. He both defines art and offers criteria for determining the quality of a given artwork. The *Poetics* stands in opposition to the theory of art propounded by Aristotle's teacher, Plato. In his *Republic,* Plato argues that "poetry is a representation of mere appearances and is thus misleading and morally suspect". In the poetics, Aristotle, Plato's student, attempts to refute his teacher by exploring what unites all poetry: its imitative nature and its ability to bring an audience into its specific plot while preserving a unity of purpose and theme. The tone of the *Poetics* reflects its argumentative spirit as Aristotle attempts both to explain the "anatomy" of poetry and to justify its value to human society.

Despite its broad goals, however, Aristotle's arguments are quite concrete. He is less interested in the abstract "existence" of art than he is in looking at specific artworks by specific playwrights. Aristotle wants to explain why effective poetry has stayed with audiences for so long. He tends to look for "empirical evidence" i.e. sensory proof through past observation that art is both good and useful, no matter how philosophers like Plato try to dismiss it.

Chapter 2

Introduction: Aristotle

Aristotle represents for most of us an icon of difficult or abstruse philosophical thinking; to know Aristotle often provokes hushed whispers even from highly educated people. For all this reputation, though, Aristotle is actually quite an easy read, for the man thought with an incredible clarity and wrote with a superhuman precision. It really is not possible to talk about Western culture (or modern, global culture) without coming to terms with this often difficult and often inspiring philosopher who didn't get along with his famous teacher, Plato, and, in fact, didn't get along with just about everybody (no-one likes a know-it-all). We can say without exaggeration that we live in an Aristotelean world; wherever you see modern, Western science dominating a culture in any meaningful way (which is just about everywhere), Aristotle is there in some form.

Aristotle was born at Stagira, in Thrace, in 384 B.C. His father was a physician to the king of Macedon, so science was in his background. At the age of seventeen, he went to Athens and joined Plato's school, where he stayed until Plato's death in 347. A few years later, he became the tutor to the young prince of Macedon, Alexander the Great. Although Alexander was a stellar pupil, Aristotle returned to Athens three years later, founded his own school, the Lyceum, and taught and studied there for twelve years. Because Alexander began conquering all of the known world, Macedonians became somewhat unwelcome in Athens and Aristotle was accordingly shown the door in 323. He died a year later.

Although he studied under Plato, Aristotle fundamentally disagreed with his teacher on just about everything. He could not bring himself to think of the world in abstract terms the way Plato did; above all else, Aristotle believed that the world could be understood at a fundamental level through the detailed observation and cataloging of phenomenon. That is, knowledge (which is what the word science means) is fundamentally empirical. As a result of this belief, Aristotle literally wrote about everything: poetics, rhetoric, ethics, politics, meteorology, embryology, physics, mathematics, metaphysics, anatomy, physiology, logic, dreams, and so forth. We aren't certain if he wrote these works directly or if they represent his or somebody else's notes on his classes; what we can say for certain is that the words, "I don't know," never came out of his mouth. In addition to studying everything, Aristotle was the first person to really think out the problem of evidence. When he approached a problem, he would examine a.) what people had previously written or said on the subject, b.) the general consensus of opinion on the subject, c.) and a systematic study of everything else that is part of or related to the subject. In his treatise on animals, he studied over five hundred species; in studying government, he collected and read 158 individual constitutions of Greek states as his fundamental data. This is called inductive reasoning: observing as many examples as possible and then working out the underlying principles. Inductive reasoning is the foundation of the Western scientific method.

Outside of the empirical method, three characteristics stand out in Aristotle's thought: the schematization of knowledge, the four causes, and the ethical doctrine of the mean.

The Classification of Knowledge. Perhaps the most fundamental aspect of Aristoteleanism is the classification of knowledge according the objects of that knowledge. The Greeks for some time had been concerned about the nature of human knowledge; this concern is called epistemology, or the "study of knowledge." For a long time, Greek philosophy dealt with questions of certainty; how could one be certain of knowledge? Suppose everything was an illusion? Aristotle resolved the question by categorizing knowledge based on their objects and the relative certainty with which you could know those objects. For instance, certain objects (such as in mathematics or logic) permit you to have a knowledge that is true all the time (two plus two always equals four). These types of knowledge are characterized by certainty and precise explanations. Other objects (such as human behaviour) don't permit certain knowledge (if you insult somebody you may not make them angry or you may make them angry). These types of knowledge are characterized by *probability* and imprecise explanations. Knowledge that would fall into this category would include ethics, psychology, or politics. Unlike Plato and Socrates, Aristotle did not demand certainty in everything. One cannot expect the same level of certainty in politics or ethics that one can demand in geometry or logic. In *Ethics* I.3, Aristotle defines the difference in the following way, "we must be satisfied to indicate the truth with a rough and general sketch: when the subject and the basis of a discussion consist of matters which hold good only as a general rule, but not always, the conclusions reached must be of the same order.... For a well-schooled man is one who searches for that degree of precision in each kind of study which the nature of the subject at hand admits: it is obviously just as foolish to accept arguments of probability from a mathematician as to demand strict demonstrations from an orator."

The Four Causes. If you walk out of this class knowing anything really well, it should be this, for Aristotle's "four causes" stand at the heart of Western rationality and Western science. In order to know a thing, anything at all, Aristotle says that one must be able to answer four questions.

Plato looked at the world and saw nothing but change; he wondered how we can know anything at all when everything is in motion and change. Plato solved the problem by postulating an unchanging world of intelligible Forms or Ideas of which our world is but an imperfect copy. But Aristotle embraced the visible world of change and motion and sought all his life to describe the principles which bring about change and motion. 1 Therefore, the question that dominated his thought at all points was: what is the cause (in Greek, *aitia,* which also means "responsible factor" 2) of this particular change or motion that I'm observing? What causes this thing to come into existence? What causes it to pass out of existence? Aristotle was the first major thinker to base his thought and science entirely on the idea that everything that moves or changes is caused to move or change by some other thing.

What causes motion and change in the universe? The four causes: a.) the material cause: the matter out of which a thing is made (clay is the material cause of a bowl); b.) the formal cause: the pattern, model, or structure upon which a thing is made (the formal cause of a bowl is "bowl-shaped"; the formal cause of a human is "human-shaped"); c.) the efficient cause: the means or agency by which a thing comes into existence (a potter is the efficient cause of a bowl); d.) the final (in Greek, *telos)* cause: the goal or purpose of a thing, its function or potential (holding cereal and milk is the final cause of a bowl). The final cause is the most unscientific, but is far and away the most important "cause" of a thing as far as Aristotle was concerned. Aristotle's analysis of phenomenon and change, then, is fundamentally teleological.

Aristotle's thought is consistently teleological: everything is always changing and moving, and has some aim, goal, or purpose *(telos)*. To borrow from a Newtonian physics, we might say that everything has potential which may be actualized (an acorn is potentially an oak tree; the process of change and motion which the acorn undertakes is directed at realizing this potential).

The Doctrine of the Mean. The Four Causes are universally applicable. However, ethics is a science that admits of a high degree of uncertainty because of the infinite variety of human actions and motivations. Now, normally ethics seems to require absolute and unchanging principles ("Thou shalt not kill") which individuals depart from at their peril. The idea that ethics are "man-made" is a problematic idea; the idea that it is the individual situation which dictates whether an action is right or wrong is, at least to early human society, downright revolutionary. But this is what Aristotle concluded and it fits in perfectly with his general empirical temperament. He works out an entire system of ethics based on the "mean" to serve as a guideline to human behaviour. There is no proper definition of any moral virtue, but rather every moral virtue stands in relationship to two opposing vices. Take courage. Courage is the opposite of cowardice. But, it is also the opposite of foolhardiness. Somewhere between foolhardiness and cowardice, that's where courage lies. What constitutes this "mean" between the two terms varies from situation to situation: what is courageous in one situation may be cowardly in another; what is foolhardy in one situation may be courageous in another. Therefore, every action needs to be judged according to all the relevant circumstances and situation. Aristotle called judging actions in this manner, "equity," and equity is the foundation of modern law and justice, and is absolutely critical in understanding foundational Christianity and its later permutations, such as the Protestant Reformation. But that's a story for another day.

Chapter 3

Aristotle: Biography

Aristotle (Greek: Αριστοτελης *Aristotélçs*) (384 BC – 322 BC) was a Greek philosopher, a student of Plato and teacher of Alexander the Great. He wrote on many different subjects, including physics, metaphysics, poetry, theater, music, logic, rhetoric, politics, gozvernment, ethics, biology and zoology. Aristotle (together with Socrates and Plato) is one of the most important founding figures in Western philosophy.

He was the first to create a comprehensive system of philosophy, encompassing morality and aesthetics, logic and science, politics and metaphysics. Aristotle's views on the physical sciences profoundly shaped medieval scholarship, and their influence extended well into the Renaissance, although they were ultimately replaced by modern physics. In the biological sciences, some of his observations were only confirmed to be accurate in the nineteenth century. His works contain the earliest known formal study of logic, which were incorporated in the late nineteenth century into modern formal logic.

In metaphysics, Aristotelianism had a profound influence on philosophical and theological thinking in the Islamic and Jewish traditions in the Middle Ages, and it continues to influence Christian theology, especially Eastern Orthodox theology, and the scholastic tradition of the Roman Catholic Church.

All aspects of Aristotle's philosophy continue to be the object of active academic study today. Though Aristotle wrote many elegant treatises and dialogues (Cicero described his literary style as "a river of gold"), it is thought that the majority of his writings are now lost; it is believed that only about one third of the original works have survived.".

Life

Aristotle was born in Stageira, Chalcidice, in 384 BC. His father was the personal physician to King Amyntas of Macedon. Aristotle was trained and educated as a member of the aristocracy. At about the age of eighteen, he went to Athens to continue his education at Plato's Academy. Aristotle remained at the academy for nearly twenty years, not leaving until after Plato's death in 347 BC.

He then traveled with Xenocrates to the court of Hermias of Atarneus in Asia Minor. While in Asia, Aristotle traveled with Theophrastus to the island of Lesbos, where together they researched the botany and zoology of the island. Aristotle married Hermias' daughter (or niece) Pythias. She bore him a daughter, whom they named Pythias. Soon after Hermias' death, Aristotle was invited by Philip of Macedon to become tutor to Alexander the Great and is said to have disciplined him by whippings.

After spending several years tutoring the young Alexander the Great, Aristotle returned to Athens. By 335 BC, he established his own school there, known as the Lyceum. Aristotle conducted courses at the school for the next twelve years. While in Athens, his wife Pythias died, and Aristotle became involved with Herpyllis of Stageira, who bore him a son whom he named after his father, Nicomachus. According to the Suda, he also had an eromenos, Palaephatus of Abydus.

It is during this period in Athens when Aristotle is believed to have composed many of his works. Aristotle wrote many dialogues, only fragments of which survived. The works that have survived are in treatise form and were not, for the most part, intended for widespread publication, as they are generally thought to be lecture aids for his students. His most important treatises include *Physics, Metaphysics, Nicomachean Ethics, Politics, De Anima (On the Soul)* and *Poetics*. These works, although connected in many fundamental ways, vary significantly in both style and substance.

Aristotle not only studied almost every subject possible at the time, but made significant contributions to most of them. In physical science, Aristotle studied anatomy, astronomy, economics, embryology, geography, geology, meteorology, physics and zoology.

In philosophy, he wrote on aesthetics, ethics, government, metaphysics, politics, psychology, rhetoric and theology. He also studied education, foreign customs, literature and poetry. His combined works constitute a virtual encyclopedia of Greek knowledge. It has been suggested that Aristotle was probably the last person to know everything there was to be known in his own time.

Upon Alexander's death, anti-Macedonian sentiment in Athens once again flared. Eurymedon the hierophant denounced Aristotle for not holding the gods in honor. Aristotle fled the city to his mother's family estate in Chalcis, explaining, "I will not allow the Athenians to sin twice against philosophy," a reference to Athens's prior trial and execution of Socrates. However, he died in Euboea of natural causes within the year (in 322 BC). Aristotle left a will and named chief executor his student Antipater, in which he asked to be buried next to his wife.

Logic

Aristotle's conception of logic was the dominant form of logic until 19th century advances in mathematical logic. Kant stated in the *Critique of Pure Reason* that Aristotle's theory of logic completely accounted for the core of deductive inference.

History

Aristotle "says that 'on the subject of reasoning' he 'had nothing else on an earlier date to speak of'". However, Plato reports that syntax was devised before him, by Prodikos of Keos, who was concerned by the correct use of words. Logic seems to have emerged from dialectics; the earlier philosophers made frequent use of concepts like *reductio ad absurdum* in their discussions, but never truly understood the logical implications.

Even Plato had difficulties with logic; although he had a reasonable conception of a deduction system, he could never actually construct one and relied instead on his dialectic, which confused science with methodology. Plato believed that deduction would simply follow from premises, hence he focused on maintaining solid premises so that the conclusion would logically follow. Consequently, Plato realized that a method for obtaining conclusions would be most beneficial. He never succeeded in devising such a method, but his best attempt was published in his book *Sophist*, where he introduced his division method.

Analytics and the Organon

What we today call *Aristotelian logic*, Aristotle himself would have labeled "analytics". The term "logic" he reserved to mean *dialectics*. Most of Aristotle's work is probably not in its original form, since it was most likely edited by students and later lecturers. The logical works of Aristotle were compiled into six books in about the early 1st century AD:

- *Categories*
- *On Interpretation*
- *Prior Analytics*
- *Posterior Analytics*
- *Topics*
- *On Sophistical Refutations*

The order of the books (or the teachings from which they are composed) is not certain, but this list was derived from analysis of Aristotle's writings.

It goes from the basics, the analysis of simple terms in the Categories, to the study of more complex forms, namely, syllogisms (in the Analytics) and dialectics (in the Topics and Sophistical Refutations). There is one volume of Aristotle's concerning logic not found in the *Organon*, namely the fourth book of *Metaphysics*.

Modal Logic

Aristotle is also the creator of syllogisms with modalities (modal logic). The word modal refers to the word 'modes', explaining the fact that modal logic deals with the modes of truth. Aristotle introduced the qualification of 'necessary' and 'possible' premises.

Aristotle's Scientific Method

Plato (left) and Aristotle (right), a detail of *The School of Athens*, a fresco by Raphael. Aristotle gestures to the earth, representing his belief in knowledge through empirical observation and experience, while holding a copy of his *Nicomachean Ethics* in his hand, whilst Plato gestures to the heavens, representing his belief in The Forms.

Like his teacher Plato, Aristotle's philosophy aims at the universal. Aristotle, however, found the universal in particular things, which he called the essence of things, while Plato finds that the universal exists apart from particular things, and is related to them as their prototype or exemplar.

For Aristotle, therefore, philosophic method implies the ascent from the study of particular phenomena to the knowledge of essences, while for Plato philosophic method means the descent from a knowledge of universal Forms (or ideas) to a contemplation of particular imitations of these. For Aristotle, "form" still refers to the unconditional basis of phenomena but is "instantiated" in a particular substance (see *Universals and particulars*, below). In a certain sense, Aristotle's method is both inductive and deductive, while Plato's is essentially deductive from *a priori* principles.

In Aristotle's terminology, "natural philosophy" is a branch of philosophy examining the phenomena of the natural world, and included fields that would be regarded today as physics, biology and other natural sciences. In modern times, the scope of *philosophy* has become limited to more generic or abstract inquiries, such as ethics and metaphysics, in which logic plays a major role.

Today's philosophy tends to exclude empirical study of the natural world by means of the scientific method. In contrast, Aristotle's philosophical endeavors encompassed virtually all facets of intellectual inquiry. In the larger sense of the word, Aristotle makes philosophy coextensive with reasoning, which he also would describe as "science". Note, however, that his use of the term *science* carries a different meaning than that covered by the term "scientific method". For Aristotle, "all science (*dianoia*) is either practical, poetical or theoretical" (*Metaphysics* 1025b25). By practical science, he means ethics and politics; by poetical science, he means the study of poetry and the other fine arts; by theoretical science, he means physics, mathematics and metaphysics.

If logic (or "analytics") is regarded as a study preliminary to philosophy, the divisions of Aristotelian philosophy would consist of: (1) Logic; (2) Theoretical Philosophy, including Metaphysics, Physics, Mathematics, (3) Practical Philosophy and (4) Poetical Philosophy.

In the period between his two stays in Athens, between his times at the Academy and the Lyceum, Aristotle conducted most of the scientific thinking and research for which he is renowned today. In fact, most of Aristotle's life was devoted to the study of the objects of natural science. Aristotle's metaphysics contains observations on the nature of numbers but he made no original contributions to mathematics. He did, however, perform original research in the natural sciences, e.g., botany, zoology, physics, astronomy, chemistry, meteorology, and several other sciences.

Aristotle's writings on science are largely qualitative, as opposed to quantitative. Beginning in the sixteenth century, scientists began applying mathematics to the physical sciences, and Aristotle's work in this area was deemed hopelessly inadequate. His failings were largely due to the absence of concepts like mass, velocity, force and temperature. He had a conception of speed and temperature, but no quantitative understanding of them, which was partly due to the absence of basic experimental devices, like clocks and thermometers.

His writings provide an account of many scientific observations, a mixture of precocious accuracy and curious errors. For example, in his *History of Animals* he claimed that human males have more teeth than females.

In a similar vein, John Philoponus, and later Galileo, showed by simple experiments that Aristotle's theory that the more massive object falls faster than a less massive object is incorrect. On the other hand, Aristotle refuted Democritus's claim that the Milky Way was made up of "those stars which are shaded by the earth from the sun's rays," pointing out (correctly, even if such reasoning was bound to be dismissed for a long time) that, given "current astronomical demonstrations" that "the size of the sun is greater than that of the earth and the distance of the stars from the earth many times greater than that of the sun, then...the sun shines on all the stars and the earth screens none of them."

In places, Aristotle goes too far in deriving 'laws of the universe' from simple observation and over-stretched reason. Today's scientific method assumes that such thinking without sufficient facts is ineffective, and that discerning the validity of one's hypothesis requires far more rigorous experimentation than that which Aristotle used to support his laws.

Aristotle also had some scientific blind spots, the largest being his inability to see the application of mathematics to physics. Aristotle held that physics was about changing objects with a reality of their own, whereas mathematics was about unchanging objects without a reality of their own. In this philosophy, he could not imagine that there was a relationship between them.

He also posited a flawed cosmology that we may discern in selections of the *Metaphysics*, which was widely accepted up until the 1500s. From the 3rd century to the 1500s, the dominant view held that the Earth was the centre of the universe (geocentrism). This scientific concept, as proposed by Aristotle and Plato was later adopted as dogma by the Roman Catholic Church because it placed mankind at the centre of the universe, and scientists who disagreed, such as Galileo, were considered heretics. This erroneous concept was eventually rejected.

Since he was perhaps the philosopher most respected by European thinkers during and after the Renaissance, these thinkers often took Aristotle's erroneous positions as given, which held back science in this epoch. However, Aristotle's scientific shortcomings should not mislead one into forgetting his great advances in the many scientific fields. For instance, he founded logic as a formal science and created foundations to biology that were not superseded (in the West) for two millennia. Moreover, he introduced the fundamental notion that nature is composed of things that change and that studying such changes can provide useful knowledge of underlying constants. This made the study of physics, and all other sciences, respectable. In actuality, however, this observation transcends physics into metaphysics.

Physics

The five Elements

- Fire, which is hot and dry.
- Earth, which is cold and dry.
- Air, which is hot and wet.
- Water, which is cold and wet.
- Aether, which is the divine substance that makes up the heavenly spheres and heavenly bodies (stars and planets).

Each of the four earthly elements has its natural place; the earth at the centre of the universe, then water, then air, then fire. When they are out of their natural place they have natural motion, requiring no external cause, which is towards that place; so bodies sink in water, air bubbles up, rain falls, flame rises in air. The heavenly element has perpetual circular motion.

Causality, The Four Causes

- The material cause is that from which a thing comes into existence as from its parts, constituents, substratum or materials. This reduces the explanation of causes to the parts (factors, elements, constituents, ingredients) forming the whole (system, structure, compound, complex, composite, or combination), a relationship known as the part-whole causation.
- The formal cause tells us what a thing is, that any thing is determined by the definition, form, pattern,

essence, whole, synthesis or archetype. It embraces the account of causes in terms of fundamental principles or general laws, as the whole (i.e., macrostructure) is the cause of its parts, a relationship known as the whole-part causation.

- The efficient cause is that from which the change or the ending of the change first starts. It identifies 'what makes of what is made and what causes change of what is changed' and so suggests all sorts of agents, nonliving or living, acting as the sources of change or movement or rest. Representing the current understanding of causality as the relation of cause and effect, this covers the modern definitions of "cause" as either the agent or agency or particular events or states of affairs.
- The final cause is that for the sake of which a thing exists or is done, including both purposeful and instrumental actions and activities. The final cause or telos is the purpose or end that something is supposed to serve, or it is that from which and that to which the change is. This also covers modern ideas of mental causation involving such psychological causes as volition, need, motivation, or motives, rational, irrational, ethical, all that gives purpose to behaviour.

Additionally, things can be causes of one another, causing each other reciprocally, as hard work causes fitness and vice versa, although not in the same way or function, the one is as the beginning of change, the other as the goal. (Thus Aristotle first suggested a reciprocal or circular causality as a relation of mutual dependence or influence of cause upon effect). Moreover, Aristotle indicated that the same thing can be the cause of contrary effects; its presence and absence may result in different outcomes. Aristotle marked two modes of causation: proper (prior) causation and accidental (chance) causation. All causes, proper and incidental, can be spoken as potential or as actual, particular or generic. The same language refers to the effects of causes, so that generic effects assigned to generic causes, particular effects to particular causes, operating causes to actual effects. Essentially, causality does not suggest a temporal relation between the cause and the effect. All further investigations of causality will consist of imposing the favourite hierarchies on the order causes, such as final > efficient > material > formal (Thomas Aquinas), or of restricting all causality to the material and efficient causes or to the efficient causality (deterministic or chance) or just to regular sequences and correlations of natural phenomena (the natural sciences describing how things happen instead of explaining the whys and wherefores).

Chance and Spontaneity

Spontaneity and chance are causes of effects. Chance as an incidental cause lies in the realm of accidental things. It is "from what is spontaneous" (but note that what is spontaneous does not come from chance). For a better understanding of Aristotle's conception of "chance" it might be better to think of "coincidence": Something takes place by chance if a person sets out with the intent of having one thing take place, but with the result of another thing (not intended) taking place.

For example: A person seeks donations. That person may find another person willing to donate a substantial sum. However, if the person seeking the donations met the person donating, not for the purpose of collecting donations, but for some other purpose, Aristotle would call the collecting of the donation by that particular donator a result of chance. It must be unusual that something happens by chance. In other words, if something happens all or most of the time, we cannot say that it is by chance. There is also more specific kind of chance, which Aristotle names "luck", that can only apply to human beings, since it is in the sphere of moral actions. According to Aristotle, luck must involve choice (and thus deliberation), and only humans are capable of deliberation and choice. "What is not capable of action cannot do anything by chance".

Metaphysics

Aristotle defines metaphysics as "the knowledge of immaterial being," or of "being in the highest degree of abstraction." He refers to metaphysics as "first philosophy", as well as "the theologic science."

Substance, Potentiality and Actuality

Aristotle examines the concept of substance (*ousia*) in his *Metaphysics*, Book VII and he concludes that a particular **substance** is a combination of both matter and form. As he proceeds to the book VIII, he concludes that the matter of the substance is the substratum or the stuff of which it is composed, *e.g.* the matter of the house are the bricks, stones, timbers etc., or whatever constitutes the *potential* house. While the form of the substance, is the *actual* house, namely 'covering for bodies and chattels' or any other differentia (see also predicables). The formula that gives the components is the account of the matter, and the formula that gives the differentia is the account of the form.

With regard to the change (*kinesis*) and its causes now, as he defines in his Physics and On Generation and Corruption 319b-320a, he distinguishes the coming to be from 1. growth and diminution, which is change in quantity 2. locomotion, which is change in space and 3. alteration, which is change in quality. The coming to be is a change where nothing persists of which the resultant is a property. In that particular change he introduces the concept of potentiality (*dynamis*) and actuality (*entelecheia*) in association with the matter and the form.

Referring to potentiality, this is what a thing is capable of doing, or being acted upon, if it is not prevented by something else. For example, the seed of a plant in the soil is potentially (*dynamei*) plant, and if is not prevented by something, it will become a plant. Potentially beings can either 'act' (*poiein*) or 'be acted upon' (*paschein*), which can be either innate or learned. For example, the eyes possess the potentiality of sight (innate - being acted upon), while the capability of playing the flute can be possessed by learning (exercise - acting).

Actuality is the fulfillment of the end of the potentiality. Because the end (*telos*) is the principle of every change, and for the sake of the end exists potentiality, therefore actuality is the end. Referring then to our previous example, we could say that actuality is when the seed of the plant becomes a plant.

" For that for the sake of which a thing is, is its principle, and the becoming is for the sake of the end; and the actuality is the end, and it is for the sake of this that the potentiality is acquired. For animals do not see in order that they may have sight, but they have sight that they may see."

In conclusion, the matter of the house is its potentiality and the form is its actuality. The formal cause (aitia) then of that change from potential to actual house, is the reason (logos) of the house builder and the final cause is the end, namely the house itself. Then Aristotle proceeds and concludes that the actuality is prior to potentiality in formula, in time and in substantiality.

With this definition of the particular substance (i.e., matter and form), Aristotle tries to solve the problem of the unity of the beings, e.g., what is that makes the man one? Since, according to Plato there are two Ideas: animal and biped, how then is man a unity? However, according to Aristotle, the potential being (matter) and the actual one (form) are one and the same thing.

Universals and Particulars

Aristotle's predecessor, Plato, argued that all things have a universal form, which could be either a property, or a relation to other things. When we look at an apple, for example, we see an apple, and we can also analyse a form of an apple. In this distinction, there is a particular apple and a universal form of an apple. Moreover, we can place an apple next to a book, so that we can speak of both the book and apple as being next to each other.

Plato argued that there are some universal forms that are not a part of particular things. For example, it is possible that there is no particular good in existence, but "good" is still a proper universal form. Bertrand Russell is a contemporary philosopher that agreed with Plato on the existence of "uninstantiated universals".

Aristotle disagreed with Plato on this point, arguing that

all universals are "instantiated". Aristotle argued that there are no universals that are unattached to existing things. According to Aristotle, if a universal exists, either as a particular or a relation, then there must have been, must be currently, or must be in the future, something on which the universal can be predicated. Consequently, according to Aristotle, if it is not the case that some universal can be predicated to an object that exists at some period of time, then it does not exist.

One way for contemporary philosophers to justify this position is by asserting the eleatic principle.

In addition, Aristotle disagreed with Plato about the location of universals. As Plato spoke of the world of the forms, a location where all universal forms subsist, Aristotle maintained that universals exist within each thing on which each universal is predicated. So, according to Aristotle, the form of apple exists within each apple, rather than in the world of the forms.

Biology and Medicine

Empirical Research Programme

Aristotle is the earliest natural historian whose work has survived in some detail. Aristotle did his research on natural history on the isle of Lesbos. The works that reflect this research, including *History of Animals, Generation of Animals,* and *Parts of Animals,* contain some remarkable observations and interpretations, along with sundry myths and mistakes. The most striking passages are about the sea-life visible from observation on Lesbos and available from the catches of fishermen. His observations on catfish, electric fish (Torpedo) and angler-fish are exceptional, as is his writing on cephalopods, molluscs, octopus, sepia (cuttlefish) and the paper nautilus (Argonauta argo). His description of the hectocotyl arm (see cephalopod) was about two thousand years ahead of its time, and widely disbelieved until its rediscovery in the nineteenth century. He separated the aquatic mammals from fish, and knew that sharks and rays were part of the group he called Selachç (selachians). He gave accurate descriptions of ruminants' four-chambered fore-stomachs, and of the unusual mammal-like embryological development of the hound shark Mustelus laevis.

Theory of Biological Being

However, for Charles Singer, "Nothing is more remarkable than [Aristotle's] efforts to [exhibit] the relationships of living things as a *scala naturae*" Aristotle's *History of Animals* classified organisms in relation to a hierarchical "Ladder of Life" (*scala naturae*), placing them according to complexity of structure and function so that higher organisms showed greater vitality and ability to move.

Aristotle believed that intellectual purposes, i.e., formal causes, guided all natural processes. Such a teleological view gave Aristotle cause to justify his observed data as an expression of formal design. Noting that "no animal has, at the same time, both tusks and horns," and "a single-hooved animal with two horns I have never seen," Aristotle suggested that Nature, giving no animal both horns and tusks, was staving off vanity, and giving creatures faculties only to such a degree as they are necessary. Noting that ruminants had a multiple stomachs and weak teeth, he supposed the first was to compensate for the latter, with Nature trying to preserve a type of balance.

In a similar fashion, Aristotle believed that creatures were arranged in a graded scale of perfection rising from plants on up to man, the *scala naturae* or Great Chain of Being. His system had eleven grades, arranged according "to the degree to which they are infected with potentiality", expressed in their form at birth. The highest animals laid warm and wet creatures alive, the lowest bore theirs cold, dry, and in thick eggs. Aristotle also held that the level of a creature's perfection was reflected in its form, but not foreordained by that form. He placed great importance on the type(s) of soul an organism possessed, asserting that plants possess a vegetative soul, responsible for reproduction and growth, animals a vegetative and a sensitive soul, responsible for mobility and sensation, and humans a vegetative, a sensitive, and a rational soul, capable of thought and reflection. Aristotle, in contrast to earlier philosophers, but in accordance with the Egyptians, placed the rational soul in the heart, rather than the brain. Notable is Aristotle's division of sensation and thought, which generally went against previous philosophers, with the exception of Alcmaeon. His analysis of procreation is frequently criticized on the grounds that it presupposes an active, ensouling masculine element bringing life to an inert, passive, lumpen female element; it is on these grounds that Aristotle is considered by some feminist critics to have been a misogynist.

Aristotle's Successor: Theophrastus

Frontispiece to a 1644 version of the expanded and illustrated edition of *Historia Plantarum* (ca. 1200), which was originally written around 200 BC Aristotle's successor at the Lyceum, Theophrastus, wrote a series of books on botany—the *History of Plants*—which survived as the most important contribution of antiquity to botany, even into the Middle Ages. Many of Theophrastus' names survive into modern times, such as *carpos* for fruit, and *pericarpion* for seed vessel. Rather than focus on formal causes, as Aristotle did, Theophrastus suggested a mechanistic scheme, drawing analogies between natural and artificial processes, and relying on Aristotle's concept of the efficient cause. Theophrastus also recognized the role of sex in the reproduction of some higher plants, though this last discovery was lost in later ages.

The Effect of Aristotle on Hellenistic Medicine

Following Theophrastus, the Lyceum failed to produce any original work. Though interest in Aristotle's ideas survived, they were generally taken unquestioningly. It is not until the age of Alexandria under the Ptolemies that advances in biology can be again found.

The first medical teacher at Alexandria Herophilus of Chalcedon, corrected Aristotle, placing intelligence in the brain, and connected the nervous system to motion and sensation. Herophilus also distinguished between veins and arteries, noting that the latter pulse while the former do not. Though a few ancient atomists such as Lucretius challenged the teleological viewpoint of Aristotelian ideas about life, teleology (and after the rise of Christianity, natural theology) would remain central to biological thought essentially until the 18th and 19th centuries. In the words of Ernst Mayr, "Nothing of any real consequence in biology after Lucretius and Galen until the Renaissance." (in Europe at least-advancement in the field continued in the Middle East and orient). Aristotle's ideas of natural history and medicine survived, but they were generally taken unquestioningly.

Practical Philosophy

Ethics

Aristotle considered ethics to be a practical science, i.e., one mastered by doing rather than merely reasoning. Further, Aristotle believed that ethical knowledge is not certain knowledge (like metaphysics and epistemology) but is general knowledge. He wrote several treatises on ethics, including most notably, *Nichomachean Ethics,* in which he outlines what is commonly called virtue ethics.

Aristotle taught that virtue has to do with the proper function of a thing. An eye is only a good eye in so much as it can see, because the proper function of an eye is sight. Aristotle reasoned that man must have a function uncommon to anything else, and that this function must be an activity of the soul.Aristotle identified the best activity of the soul as eudaimonia: a happiness or joy that pervades the good life. Aristotle taught that to achieve the good life, one must live a balanced life and avoid excess. This balance, he taught, varies among different persons and situations, and exists as a golden mean between two vices - one an excess and one a deficiency.

Politics

In addition to his works on ethics, which address the individual, Aristotle addressed the city in his work titled

Politics. Aristotle's conception of the city is very organic, and he is considered one of the first to conceive of the city in this manner. Aristotle considered the city to be a natural community.

Moreover, he considered the city to be prior to the family which in turn is prior to the individual, i.e., last in the order of becoming, but first in the order of being (1253a19-24). He is also famous for his statement that "man is by nature a political animal." Aristotle conceived of politics as being rather like an organism than like a machine, and as a collection of parts that cannot exist without the other.

It should be noted that the modern understanding of a political community is that of the state. However, the state was foreign to Aristotle. He referred to political communities as cities. Aristotle understood a city as a political "partnership" (1252a1) and not one of a social contract (or compact) or a political community as understood by Niccolò Machiavelli. Subsequently, a city is created not to avoid injustice or for economic stability (1280b29-31), but rather to live a good life: "The political partnership must be regarded, therefore, as being for the sake of noble actions, not for the sake of living together" (1281a1-3). This can be distinguished from the social contract theory which individuals leave the state of nature because of "fear of violent death" or its "inconveniences."

Rhetoric and Poetics

Aristotle considered epic poetry, tragedy, comedy, dithyrambic poetry and music to be imitative, each varying in imitation by media, object, and manner. For example, music imitates with the media of rhythm and harmony, whereas dance imitates with rhythm alone, and poetry with language. The forms also differ in their object of imitation.

Comedy, for instance, is a dramatic imitation of men worse than average; whereas tragedy imitates men slightly better than average. Lastly, the forms differ in their manner of imitation - through narrative or character, through change or no change, and through drama or no drama. Aristotle believed that imitiation is natural to mankind and constitutes one of mankind's advantages over animals. While it is believed that Aristotle's *Poetics* was comprised of two books - one on comedy and one on tragedy - only the portion that focuses on tragedy has survived. Aristotle taught that tragedy is composed of six elements: plot-structure, character, style, spectacle, and lyric poetry.

The characters in a tragedy are merely a means of driving the story; and the plot, not the characters, is the chief focus of tragedy. Tragedy is the imitation of action arousing pity and fear, and is meant to effect the catharsis of those same emotions. Aristotle concludes *Poetics* with a discussion on which, if either, is superior: epic or tragic mimesis. He suggest that because tragedy possesses all the attributes of an epic, possibly possesses additional attributes such as spectacle and music, is more unified, and achieves the aim of its mimesis in shorter scope, it can be considered superior to epic.

The Loss of his Works

According to a distinction that originates with Aristotle himself, his writings are divisible into two groups: the "exoteric" and the "esoteric". Most scholars have understood this as a distiction between works Aristotle intended for the public (exoteric), and the more technical works (esoteric) intended for the narrower audience of Aristotle's students and other philosophers who were familiar with the jargon and issues typical of the Platonic and Aristotelian schools. Another common assumption is that none of the exoteric works is extant - that all of Aristotle's extant writings are of the esoteric kind.

Current knowledge of what exactly the exoteric writings were like is scant and dubious, though many of them may have been in dialogue form. (*Fragments* of some of Aristotle's dialogues have survived.) Perhaps it is to these that Cicero refers when he characterized Aristotle's writing style as "a river of gold"; it is hard for many modern readers to accept that one could seriously so admire the style of those works currently available to us.

However, some modern scholars have warned that we cannot know for certain that Cicero's praise was reserved specifically for the exoteric works; a few modern scholars have actually admired the concise writing style found in Aristotle's extant works. One major question in the history of Aristotle's works, then, is how were the exoteric writings all lost, and how did the ones we now possess come to us? The story of the original manuscripts of the esoteric treatises is described by Strabo in his *Geography* and Plutarch in his *Parallel Lives*. The manuscripts were left from Aristotle to his successor Theophrastus, who in turn willed them to Neleus of Scepsis. Neleus supposedly took the writings from Athens to Scepsis, where his heirs let them languish in a cellar until the first century BC, when Apellicon of Teos discovered and purchased the manuscripts, bringing them back to Athens.

According to the story, Apellicon tried to repair some of the damage that was done during the manuscripts' stay in the basement, introducing a number of errors into the text. When Lucius Cornelius Sulla occupied Athens in 86 BC, he carried off the library of Apellicon to Rome, where they were first published in 60 BC by the grammarian Tyrranion of Amisus and then by philosopher Andronicus of Rhodes.

Carnes Lord attributes the popular belief in this story to the fact that it provides "the most plausible explanation for the rapid eclipse of the Peripatetic school after the middle of the third century, and for the absence of widespread knowledge of the specialized treatises of Aristotle throughout the Hellenistic period, as well as for the sudden reappearance of a flourishing Aristotelianism during the first century B.C." Lord voices a number of reservations concerning this story, however. First, the condition of the texts is far too good for them to have suffered considerable damage followed by Apellicon's inexpert attempt at repair. Second, there is "incontrovertible evidence," Lord says, that the treatises were in circulation during the time in which Strabo and Plutarch suggest they were confined within the cellar in Scepsis. Third, the definitive edition of Aristotle's texts seems to have been made in Athens some fifty years before Andronicus supposedly compiled his. And fourth, ancient library catalogues predating Andronicus' intervention list an

Aristotelean corpus quite similar to the one we currently possess. Lord sees a number of post-Aristotelean interpolations in the *Politics,* for example, but is generally confident that the work has come down to us relatively intact. After the Roman period, Aristotle's works were by and large lost to the West for a second time. They were, however, preserved in the East by various Muslim scholars and philosophers, many of whom wrote extensive commentaries on his works. Aristotle lay at the foundation of the *falsafa* movement in Islamic philosophy, stimulating the thought of Al-Farabi, Ibn Sina, Ibn Rushd and others. As the influence of the *falsafa* grew in the West, in part due to Gerard of Cremona's translations and the spread of Averroism, the demand for Aristotle's works grew. William of Moerbeke translated a number of them into Latin. When Thomas Aquinas wrote his theology, working from Moerbeke's translations, the demand for Aristotle's writings grew and the Greek manuscripts returned to the West, stimulating a revival of Aristotelianism in Europe, and ultimately revitalizing European thought through Muslim influence in Spain to fan the embers of the Renaissance.

Legacy

Early Islamic portrayal of Aristotle: Aristotle portrayed in the 1493 *Nuremberg Chronicle* as a 15th-century-A.D. scholar.

It is the opinion of many that Aristotle's system of thought remains the most influential one ever put together by any single mind. According to historian Will Durant, no other philosopher has contributed so much to the enlightenment of the world. He single-handedly founded the sciences of Logic, Biology and Psychology. At the opposite pole, Bertrand Russell dismissed much of Aristotle's work as not particularly profound. The immediate influence of Aristotle's work was felt as the Lyceum grew into the Peripatetic school. Aristotle's notable students included Aristoxenus, Dicaearchus, Demetrius of Phalerum, Eudemos of Rhodes, Harpalus, Hephaestion, Meno, Mnason of Phocis, Nicomachus, and Theophrastus. (Alexander the Great's tutelage under Aristotle should also be mentioned here, though it is unclear what the influence of this relationship was.) Aristotle is referred to as "The Philosopher" by Scholastic thinkers such as Thomas Aquinas. See *Summa Theologica,* Part I, Question 3, etc.

These thinkers blended Aristotelian philosophy with Christianity, bringing the thought of Ancient Greece into the Middle Ages. It required a repudiation of some Aristotelian principles for the sciences and the arts to free themselves for the discovery of modern scientific laws and empirical methods. The medieval English poet Chaucer describes his student as being happy by having,

At his bedded hed
Twenty books clothed in blake or red
Of Aristotle and his philosophie
The Italian poet Dante says
of Aristotle in the first circles of hell,
I saw the Master there of those who know,
Amid the philosophic family,
By all admired, and by all reverenced;
There Plato too I saw, and Socrates,
Who stood beside him closer than the rest.

The German philosopher Friedrich Nietzsche has been said to have taken nearly all of his political philosophy from Aristotle. However implausible this is, it is certainly the case that Aristotle's rigid separation of action from production, and his justification of the subservience of slaves and others to the virtue - or *arete* - of a few justified the ideal of aristocracy. It is Martin Heidegger, not Nietzsche, who elaborated a new interpretation of Aristotle, intended to warrant his deconstruction of scholastic and philosophical tradition. More recently, Alasdair MacIntyre has attempted to reform what he calls the Aristotelian tradition in a way that is anti-elitist and capable of disputing the claims of both liberals and Nietzscheans. The philosopher novelist, Ayn Rand, commented that in writing Atlas Shrugged the only philosopher to whom she could acknowledge a debt was Aristotle.

Chapter 4

Greek Theory of Tragedy: Aristotle's Poetics

The classic discussion of Greek tragedy is Aristotle's *Poetics*. He defines tragedy as "the imitation of an action that is serious and also as having magnitude, complete in itself." He continues, "Tragedy is a form of drama exciting the emotions of pity and fear.

Its action should be single and complete, presenting a reversal of fortune, involving persons renowned and of superior attainments, and it should be written in poetry embellished with every kind of artistic expression." The writer presents "incidents arousing pity and fear, wherewith to interpet its catharsis of such of such emotions" (by *catharsis*, Aristotle means a purging or sweeping away of the pity and fear aroused by the tragic action).

The basic difference Aristotle draws between tragedy and other genres, such as comedy and the epic, is the "tragic pleasure of pity and fear" the audience feel watching a tragedy. In order for the tragic hero to arouse these feelings in the audience, he cannot be either all good or all evil but must be someone the audience can identify with; however, if he is superior in some way(s), the tragic pleasure is intensified. His disastrous end results from a mistaken action, which in turn arises from a tragic flaw or from a tragic error in judgment. Often the tragic flaw is *hubris*, an excessive pride that causes the hero to ignore a divine warning or to break a moral law. It has been suggested that because the tragic hero's suffering is greater than his offense, the audience feels pity; because the audience members perceive that they could behave similarly, they feel pity.

Medieval Tragedy and the Wheel of Fortune

The medieval tragedy is a prose or poetic narrative, not a drama. Tragedy was perceived as a reversal of fortune, a fall from a high position. This view of tragedy derives from the Medieval concept of fortune, which was personified as Dame Fortune, a blindfolded woman who turned a wheel at whim; men were stationed at various places on the wheel—the top of the wheel represented the best fortune, being under the wheel the worst fortune. However, the wheel could turn suddenly and the man on top could suddenly be under the wheel, without warning.

Elizabethan and Shakespearean Tragedy

A distinctly English form of tragedy begins with the Elizabethans. The translation of Seneca and the reading of Aristotle's *Poetics* were major influences. Many critics and playwrights, such as Ben Jonson, insisted on observing the classical unities of action, time and place (the action should be one whole and take place in one day and in one place). However, it was romantic tragedy, which Shakespeare wrote in *Richard II, Macbeth, Hamlet,* and *King Lear,* which prevailed. Romantic tragedy disregarded the unities (as in the use of subplots), mixed tragedy and comedy, and emphasized action, spectacle, and—increasingly—sensation. Shakespeare violated the unities in these ways and also in mixing poetry and prose and using the device of a play-within-a-play, as in *Hamlet*. The Elizabethans and their Jacobean successsors acted on stage the violence that the Greek dramatists reported. The Elizabethan and later the Jacobean playwright had a diverse audience to please, ranging from Queen Elizabeth and King James I and their courtiers to the lowest classes.

Christopher Marlowe's tragedies showed the resources of the English language with his magnificent blank verse, as in the *Tragedy of Dr. Faustus,* and the powerful effects that could be achieved by focusing on a towering protagonist, as in

Tamburlaine. In Elizabethan tragedy, the individual leads to violence and conflict. A distinctly non-Aristotelian form of tragedy developed during this period was the tragicomedy. In a tragicomedy, the action and subject matter seem to require a tragic ending, but it is avoided by a reversal which leads to a happy ending; sometimes the tragicomedy alternates serious and comic actions throughout the play. Because it blends tragedy and comedy, the tragicomedy is sometimes referred to as a "mixed" kind.

The Problem Play or Drama of Ideas

The problem play or play of ideas usually has a tragic ending. The driving force behind the play is the exploration of some social problem, like alcoholism or prostitution; the characters are used as examples of the general problem. Frequently the playwright views the problem and its solution in a way that defies or rejects the conventional view; not surprisingly, some problem plays have aroused anger and controversy in audiences and critics. Henrik Ibsen, who helped to revive tragedy from its artistic decline in the nineteenth century, wrote problem plays. *A Doll's House,* for example, shows the exploitation and denigration of middle class women by society and in marriage. The tragedy frequently springs from the individual's conflict with the laws, values, traditions, and representatives of society.

Chapter 5

Aristotle's Poetics: Interpretation

Aristotle's *Poetics* is a much-disdained book. So unpoetic a soul as Aristotle's has no business speaking about such a topic, much less telling poets how to go about their business. He reduces the drama to its language, people say, and the language itself to its least poetic element, the story, and then he encourages insensitive readers like himself to subject stories to crudely moralistic readings, that reduce tragedies to the childish proportions of Aesop-fables. Strangely, though, the *Poetics* itself is rarely read with the kind of sensitivity its critics claim to possess, and the thing criticized is not the book Aristotle wrote but a caricature of it. Aristotle himself respected Homer so much that he personally corrected a copy of the *Iliad* for his student Alexander, who carried it all over the world. In his *Rhetoric* (III, xvi, 9), Aristotle criticizes orators who write exclusively from the intellect, rather than from the heart, in the way Sophocles makes Antigone speak. Aristotle is often thought of as a logician, but he regularly uses the adverb *logikôs*, logically, as a term of reproach contrasted with *phusikôs*, naturally or appropriately, to describe arguments made by others, or preliminary and inadequate arguments of his own. Those who take the trouble to look at the *Poetics* closely will find, I think, a book that treats its topic appropriately and naturally, and contains the reflections of a good reader and characteristically powerful thinker.

Poetry as Imitation

The first scandal in the *Poetics* is the initial marking out of dramatic poetry as a form of imitation. We call the poet a creator, and are offended at the suggestion that he might be merely some sort of recording device. As the painter's eye teaches us how to look and shows us what we never saw, the dramatist presents things that never existed until he imagined them, and makes us experience worlds we could never have found the way to on our own. But Aristotle has no intention to diminish the poet, and in fact says the same thing I just said, in making the point that poetry is more philosophic than history. By imitation, Aristotle does not mean the sort of mimicry by which Aristophanes, say, finds syllables that approximate the sound of frogs.

He is speaking of the imitation of action, and by action he does not mean mere happenings. Aristotle speaks extensively of praxis in the *Nicomachean Ethics*. It is not a word he uses loosely, and in fact his use of it in the definition of tragedy recalls the discussion in the *Ethics*. Action, as Aristotle uses the word, refers only to what is deliberately chosen, and capable of finding completion in the achievement of some purpose. Animals and young children do not act in this sense, and action is not the whole of the life of any of us. The poet must have an eye for the emergence of action in human life, and a sense for the actions that are worth paying attention to. They are not present in the world in such a way that a video camera could detect them.

An intelligent, feeling, shaping human soul must find them. By the same token, the action of the drama itself is not on the stage. It takes form and has its being in the imagination of the spectator.

The actors speak and move and gesture, but it is the poet who speaks through them, from imagination to imagination, to present to us the thing that he has made. Because that thing he makes has the form of an action, it has to be seen and held together just as actively and attentively by us as by him. The imitation is the thing that is re-produced, in us and for us, by his art. This is a powerful kind of human communication, and the thing imitated is what defines the human realm. If no one had the power to imitate action, life might just wash over us without leaving any trace.

How do I know that Aristotle intends the imitation of action to be understood in this way? In *De Anima*, he distinguishes three kinds of perception (II, 6; III, 3). There is the perception of proper sensibles-colours, sounds, tastes and so on; these lie on the surfaces of things and can be mimicked directly for sense perception. But there is also perception of common sensibles, available to more than one of our senses, as shape is grasped by both sight and touch, or number by all five senses; these are distinguished by imagination, the power in us that is shared by the five senses, and in which the circular shape, for instance, is not dependent on sight or touch alone. These common sensibles can be mimicked in various ways, as when I draw a messy, meandering ridge of chalk on a blackboard, and your imagination grasps a circle. Finally, there is the perception of that of which the sensible qualities are attributes, the thing—the son of Diares, for example; it is this that we ordinarily mean by perception, and while its object always has an image in the imagination, it can only be distinguished by intellect, *no°s* (III,4). Skilled mimics can imitate people we know, by voice, gesture, and so on, and here already we must engage intelligence and imagination together.

The dramatist imitates things more remote from the eye and ear than familiar people. Sophocles and Shakespeare, for example, imitate repentance and forgiveness, true instances of action in Aristotle's sense of the word, and we need all the human powers to recognize what these poets put before us. So the mere phrase *imitation of an action* is packed with meaning, available to us as soon as we ask what an action is, and how the image of such a thing might be perceived.

Aristotle does understand tragedy as a development out of the child's mimicry of animal noises, but that is in the same way that he understands philosophy as a development out of our enjoyment of sight-seeing (*Metaphysics* I, 1). In each of these developments there is a vast array of possible intermediate stages, but just as philosophy is the ultimate form of the innate desire to know, tragedy is considered by Aristotle the ultimate form of our innate delight in imitation. His beloved Homer saw and achieved the most important possibilities of the imitation of human action, but it was the tragedians who, refined and intensified the form of that imitation, and discovered its perfection.

The Character of Tragedy

A work is a tragedy, Aristotle tells us, only if it arouses pity and fear. Why does he single out these two passions? Some interpreters think he means them only as examples—pity and fear and other passions like that—but I am not among those loose constructionists. Aristotle does use a word that means passions of that sort (*toiouta*), but I think he does so only to indicate that pity and fear are not themselves things subject to identification with pin-point precision, but that each refers to a range of feeling. It is just the feelings in those two ranges, however, that belong to tragedy. Why? Why shouldn't some tragedy arouse pity and joy, say, and another fear and cruelty? In various places, Aristotle says that it is the mark of an educated person to know what needs explanation and what doesn't.

He does not try to prove that there is such a thing as nature, or such a thing as motion, though some people deny both. Likewise, he understands the recognition of a special and powerful form of drama built around pity and fear as the beginning of an inquiry, and spends not one word justifying that restriction. We, however, can see better why he starts there by trying out a few simple alternatives.

Suppose a drama aroused pity in a powerful way, but aroused no fear at all. This is an easily recognizable dramatic form, called a tear-jerker. The name is meant to disparage this sort of drama, but why? Imagine a well written, well made play or movie that depicts the losing struggle of a likable central character. We are moved to have a good cry, and are afforded either the relief of a happy ending, or the realistic desolation of a sad one.

In the one case the tension built up along the way is released within the experience of the work itself; in the other it passes off as we leave the theater, and readjust our feelings to the fact that it was, after all, only make-believe. What is wrong with that? There is always pleasure in strong emotion, and the theater is a harmless place to indulge it. We may even come out feeling good about being so compassionate. But Dostoyevski depicts a character who loves to cry in the theater, not noticing that while she wallows in her warm feelings her coach-driver is shivering outside. She has day-dreams about relieving suffering humanity, but does nothing to put that vague desire to work. If she is typical, then the tear-jerker is a dishonest form of drama, not even a harmless diversion but an encouragement to lie to oneself.

Well then, let's consider the opposite experiment, in which a drama arouses fear in a powerful way, but arouses little or no pity. This is again a readily recognizable dramatic form, called the horror story, or in a recent fashion, the mad-slasher movie. The thrill of fear is the primary object of such amusements, and the story alternates between the build-up of apprehension and the shock of violence.

Again, as with the tear-jerker, it doesn't much matter whether it ends happily or with uneasiness, or even with one last shock, so indeterminate is its form. And while the tearjerker gives us an illusion of compassionate delicacy, the unrestrained shock-drama obviously has the effect of coarsening feeling. Genuine human pity could not co-exist with the so-called graphic effects these films use to keep scaring us. The attraction of this kind of amusement is again the thrill of strong feeling, and again the price of indulging the desire for that thrill may be high.

Let us consider a milder form of the drama built on arousing fear. There are stories in which fearsome things are threatened or done by characters who are in the end defeated by means similar to, or in some way equivalent to, what they dealt out. The fear is relieved in vengeance, and we feel a satisfaction that we might be inclined to call justice. To work on the level of feeling, though, justice must be understood as the exact inverse of the crime—doing to the offender the sort of thing he did or meant to do to others.

The imagination of evil then becomes the measure of good, or at least of the restoration of order. The satisfaction we feel in the vicarious infliction of pain or death is nothing but a thin veil over the very feelings we mean to be punishing. This is a successful dramatic formula, arousing in us destructive desires that are fun to feel, along with the self-righteous illusion that we are really superior to the character who displays them. The playwright who makes us feel that way will probably be popular, but he is a menace.

We have looked at three kinds of non-tragedy that arouse passions in a destructive way, and we could add others. There are potentially as many kinds as there are passions and combinations of passions. That suggests that the theater is just an arena for the manipulation of passions in ways that are pleasant in the short run and at least reckless to pursue repeatedly. At worst, the drama could be seen as dealing in a kind of addiction, which it both produces and holds the only remedy for. But we have not yet tried to talk about the combination of passions characteristic of tragedy.

When we turn from the sort of examples I have given, to the acknowledged examples of tragedy, we find ourselves in a different world. The tragedians I have in mind are five: Aeschylus, Sophocles, and Euripides; Shakespeare, who differs from them only in time; and Homer, who differs from them somewhat more, in the form in which he composed, but shares with them the things that matter most. I could add other authors, such as Dostoyevski, who wrote stories of the tragic kind in much looser literary forms, but I want to keep the focus on a small number of clear paradigms.

When we look at a tragedy we find the chorus in Antigone telling us what a strange thing a human being is, that passes beyond all boundaries (lines 332 ff.), or King Lear asking if man is no more than this, a poor, bare, forked animal (III, iv, 97ff.), or Macbeth protesting to his wife "I dare do all that may become a man; who dares do more is none" (I, vii, 47-8), or Oedipus taunting Teiresias with the fact that divine art was of no use against the Sphinx, but only Oedipus' own human ingenuity (*Oed. Tyr.* 39098), or Agamemnon, resisting walking home on tapestries, saying to his wife "I tell you to revere me as a man, not a god" , or Cadmus in the Bacchae saying "I am a man, nothing more", while Dionysus tells Pentheus "You do not know what you are" , or Patroclus telling Achilles "Peleus was not your father nor Thetis your mother, but the gray sea bore you, and the towering rocks, so hard is your heart" (*Iliad* XVI, 335). I could add more examples of this kind by the dozen, and your memories will supply others. Tragedy seems always to involve testing or finding the limits of what is human. This is no mere orgy of strong feeling, but a highly focussed way of bringing our powers to bear on the image of what is human as such. I suggest that Aristotle is right in saying that the powers which first of all bring this human image to sight for us are pity and fear. It is obvious that the authors in our examples are not just putting things in front of us to make us cry or shiver or gasp. The feelings they arouse are subordinated to another effect. Aristotle begins by saying that tragedy arouses pity and fear in such a way as to culminate in a cleansing of those passions, the famous catharsis. The word is used by Aristotle only the once, in his preliminary definition of tragedy. I think this is because its role is taken over later in the *Poetics* by another, more positive, word, but the idea of catharsis is important in itself, and we should consider what it might mean.

Tragic Catharsis

First of all, the tragic catharsis might be a purgation. Fear can obviously be an insidious thing that undermines life and poisons it with anxiety. It would be good to flush this feeling from our systems, bring it into the open, and clear the air. This may explain the appeal of horror movies, that they redirect our fears toward something external, grotesque, and finally ridiculous, in order to puncture them. On the other hand, fear might have a secret allure, so that what we need to purge is the desire for the thrill that comes with fear. The horror movie also provides a safe way to indulge and satisfy the longing to feel afraid, and go home afterward satisfied; the desire is purged, temporarily, by being fed. Our souls are so many-headed that opposite satisfactions may be felt at the same time, but I think these two really are opposite. In the first sense of purgation, the horror movie is a kind of medicine that does its work and leaves the soul healthier, while in the second sense it is a potentially addictive drug. Either explanation may account for the popularity of these movies among teenagers, since fear is so much a fact of that time of life. For those of us who are older, the tear-jerker may have more appeal, offering a way to purge the regrets of our lives in a sentimental outpouring of pity. As with fear, this purgation too may be either medicinal or drug-like.

This idea of purgation, in its various forms, is what we usually mean when we call something cathartic. People speak of watching football, or boxing, as a catharsis of violent urges, or call a shouting match with a friend a useful catharsis of buried resentment. This is a practical purpose that drama may also serve, but it has no particular connection with beauty or truth; to be good in this purgative way, a drama has no need to be good in any other way. No one would be tempted to confuse the feeling at the end of a horror movie with what Aristotle calls "the tragic pleasure," nor to call such a movie a tragedy. But the English word catharsis does not contain everything that is in the Greek word. Let us look at other things it might mean.

Catharsis in Greek can mean purification. While purging something means getting rid of it, purifying something means getting rid of the worse or baser parts of it. It is possible that tragedy purifies the feelings themselves of fear and pity. These arise in us in crude ways, attached to all sorts of objects. Perhaps the poet educates our sensibilities, our powers to feel and be moved, by refining them and attaching them to less easily discernible objects.

There is a line in *The Wasteland*, "I will show you fear in a handful of dust." Alfred Hitchcock once made us all feel a little shudder when we took showers. The poetic imagination is limited only by its skill, and can turn any object into a focus for any feeling.

Some people turn to poetry to find delicious and exquisite new ways to feel old feelings, and consider themselves to enter in that way into a purified state. It has been argued that this sort of thing is what tragedy and the tragic pleasure are all about, but it doesn't match up with my experience. Sophocles does make me fear and pity human knowledge when I watch the *Oedipus Tyrannus,* but this is not a refinement of those feelings but a discovery that they belong to a surprising object. Sophocles is not training my feelings, but using them to show me something worthy of wonder.

The word *catharsis* drops out of the *Poetics* because the word wonder, *to rhaumaston,* replaces it, first in chapter 9, where Aristotle argues that pity and fear arise most of all where wonder does, and finally in chapters 24 and 25, where he singles out wonder as the aim of the poetic art itself, into which the aim of tragedy in particular merges. Ask yourself how you feel at the end of a tragedy. You have witnessed horrible things and felt painful feelings, but the mark of tragedy is that it brings you out the other side. Aristotle's use of the word *catharsis* is not a technical reference to purgation or purification but a beautiful metaphor for the peculiar tragic pleasure, the feeling of being washed or cleansed.

The tragic pleasure is a paradox. As Aristotle says, in a tragedy, a happy ending doesn't make us happy. At the end of the play the stage is often littered with bodies, and we feel cleansed by it all. Are we like Clytemnestra, who says she rejoiced when spattered by her husband's blood, like the earth in a Spring rain ? Are we like Iago, who has to see a beautiful life destroyed to feel better about himself ? We all feel a certain glee in the bringing low of the mighty, but this is in no way similar to the feeling of being washed in wonderment. The closest thing I know to the feeling at the end of a tragedy is the one that comes with the sudden, unexpected appearance of something beautiful. In a famous essay on beauty, Plotinus says two things that seem true to me: "Clearly [beauty] is something detected at a first glance, something that the soul... recognizes, gives welcome to, and, in a way, fuses with" (beginning sec. 2). What is the effect on us of this recognition? Plotinus says that in every instance it is "an astonishment, a delicious wonderment" (end sec. 4). Aristotle is insistent that a tragedy must be whole and one, because only in that way can it be beautiful, while he also ascribes the superiority of tragedy over epic poetry to its greater unity and concentration (ch. 26). Tragedy is not just a dramatic form in which some works are beautiful and others not; tragedy is itself a species of beauty. All tragedies are beautiful. By following Aristotle's lead, we have now found five marks of tragedy:

- It imitates an action,
- It arouses pity and fear,
- It displays the human image as such,
- It ends in wonder,
- It is inherently beautiful. We noticed earlier that it is action that characterizes the distinctively human realm, and it is reasonable that the depiction of an action might show us a human being in some definitive way, but what do pity and fear have to do with that showing? The answer is everything.

Tragic Pity

First, let us consider what tragic pity consists in. The word pity tends to have a bad name these days, and to imply an attitude of condescension that diminishes its object. This is not a matter of the meanings of words, or even of changing attitudes. It belongs to pity itself to be two-sided, since any feeling of empathy can be given a perverse twist by the recognition that it is not oneself but another with whom one is feeling a shared pain. One of the most empathetic characters in all literature is Edgar in *King Lear*. He describes himself truly as "a most poor man, made tame to fortune's blows, Who, by the art of known and feeling sorrows, Am pregnant to good pity" (IV, vi, 217-19). Two of his lines spoken to his father are powerful evidence of the insight that comes from suffering oneself and taking on the suffering of others: "Thy life's a miracle" (IV, vi, 5 5), he says, and "Ripeness is all" (V, ii, 11), trying to help his father see that life is still good and death is not something to be sought. Yet in the last scene of the play this same Edgar voices the stupidest words ever spoken in any tragedy, when he concludes that his father just got what he deserved when he lost his eyes, since he had once committed adultery (V, iii, 171-4). Having witnessed the play, we know that Gloucester lost his eyes because he chose to help Lear, when the kingdom had become so corrupt that his act of kindness appeared as a walking fire in a dark world (III, iv, 107). There is a chain of effects from Gloucester's adultery to his mutilation, but it is not a sequence that reveals the true cause of that horror. The wholeness of action that Shakespeare shapes for us shows that Gloucester's goodness, displayed in a courageous, deliberate choice, and not his weakness many years earlier, cost him his eyes. Edgar ends by giving in to the temptation to moralize, to chase after the "fatal flaw" which is no part of tragedy, and loses his capacity to see straight.

This suggests that holding on to proper pity leads to seeing straight, and that seems exactly right. But what is proper pity? There is a way of missing the mark that is opposite to condescension, and that is the excess of pity called sentimentality. There are people who use the word *sentimental* for any display of feeling, or any taking seriously of feeling, but their attitude is as blind as Edgar's. Sentimentality is inordinate feeling, feeling that goes beyond the source that gives rise to it. The woman in Dostoyevski's novel who loves pitying for its own sake is an example of this vice. But between Edgar's moralizing and her gushing there is a range of appropriate pity. Pity is one of the instruments by which a poet can show us what we are. We pity the loss of Gloucester's eyes because we know the value of eyes, but more deeply, we pity the violation of Gloucester's decency, and in so doing we feel the truth that without such decency, and without respect for it, there is no human life. Shakespeare is in control here, and the feeling he produces does not give way in embarrassment to moral judgment, nor does it make us wallow mindlessly in pity because it feels so good; the pity he arouses in us shows us what is precious in us, in the act of its being violated in another.

Tragic Fear and the Image of Humanity

Since every boundary has two sides, the human image is

delineated also from the outside, the side of the things that threaten it. This is shown to us through the feeling of fear. As Aristotle says twice in the *Rhetoric,* what we pity in others, we fear for ourselves (1382b 26, 1386a 27). In our mounting fear that Oedipus will come to know the truth about himself, we feel that something of our own is threatened. Tragic fear, exactly like tragic pity, and either preceding it or simultaneous with it, shows us what we are and are unwilling to lose. It makes no sense to say that Oedipus' passion for truth is a flaw, since that is the very quality that makes us afraid on his behalf. Tragedy is never about flaws, and it is only the silliest of mistranslations that puts that claim in Aristotle's mouth. Tragedy is about central and indispensable human attributes, disclosed to us by the pity that draws us toward them and the fear that makes us recoil from what threatens them.

Because the suffering of the tragic figure displays the boundaries of what is human, every tragedy carries the sense of universality. Oedipus or Antigone or Lear or Othello is somehow every one of us, only more so. But the mere mention of these names makes it obvious that they are not generalized characters, but altogether particular. And if we did not feel that they were genuine individuals, they would have no power to engage our emotions.

It is by their particularity that they make their marks on us, as though we had encountered them in the flesh. It is only through the particularity of our feelings that our bonds with them emerge. What we care for and cherish makes us pity them and fear for them, and thereby the reverse also happens: our feelings of pity and fear make us recognize what we care for and cherish. When the tragic figure is destroyed it is a piece of ourselves that is lost.

Yet we never feel desolation at the end of a tragedy, because what is lost is also, by the very same means, found. I am not trying to make a paradox, but to describe a marvel. It is not so strange that we learn the worth of something by losing it; what is astonishing is what the tragedians are able to achieve by making use of that common experience. They lift it up into a state of wonder.

Within our small group of exemplary poetic works, there are two that do not have the tragic form, and hence do not concentrate all their power into putting us in a state of wonder, but also depict the state of wonder among their characters and contain speeches that reflect on it. They are Homer's *Iliad* and Shakespeare's *Tempest*. (Incidentally, there is an excellent small book called *Woe or Wonder, the Emotional Effect of Shakespearean Tragedy*, by J. V. Cunningham, that demonstrates the continuity of the traditional understanding of tragedy from Aristotle to Shakespeare.) The first poem in our literary heritage, and Shakespeare's last play, both belong to a conversation of which Aristotle's *Poetics* is the most prominent part.

The Iliad, the Tempest, and Tragic Wonder

In both the *Iliad* and the *Tempest* there are characters with arts that in some ways resemble that of the poet. It is much noticed that Prospero's farewell to his art coincides with Shakespeare's own, but it may be less obvious that Homer has put into the *Iliad* a partial representation of himself. But the last 150 lines of Book XVIII of the *Iliad* describe the making of a work of art by Hephaestus. I will not consider here what is depicted on the shield of Achilles, but only the meaning in the poem of the shield itself. In Book XVIII, Achilles has realized what mattered most to him when it is too late. The Greeks are driven back to their ships, as Achilles had prayed they would be, and know that they are lost without him. "But what pleasure is this to me now," he says to his mother, "when my beloved friend is dead, Patroclus, whom I cherished beyond all friends, as the equal of my own soul; I am bereft of him" . Those last words also mean "I have killed him." In his desolation, Achilles has at last chosen to act. "I will accept my doom," he says . Thetis goes to Hephaestus because, in spite of his resolve, Achilles has no armor in which to meet his fate. She tells her son's story, concluding "he is lying on the ground, anguishing at heart" . Her last word, anguishing, acheuôn, is built on Achilles' name.

Now listen to what Hephaestus says in reply: "Take courage, and do not let these things distress you in your heart.

Would that I had the power to hide him far away from death and the sounds of grief when grim fate comes to him, but I can see that beautiful armor surrounds him, of such a kind that many people, one after another, who look on it, will wonder". Is it not evident that this source of wonder that surrounds Achilles, that takes the sting from his death even in a mother's heart, is the *Iliad* itself? But how does the *Iliad* accomplish this?

Let us shift our attention for a moment to the *Tempest*. The character Alonso, in the power of the magician Prospero, spends the length of the play in the illusion that his son has drowned. To have him alive again, Alonso says, "I wish Myself were mudded in that oozy bed Where my son lies". But he has already been there for three hours in his imagination; he says earlier "my son i' th' ooze is bedded; and I'll seek him deeper than e'er plummet sounded And with him there lie mudded".

What is this muddy ooze? It is Alonso's grief, and his regret for exposing his son to danger, and his self-reproach for his own past crime against Prospero and Prospero's baby daughter, which made his son a just target for divine retribution; the ooze is Alonso's repentance, which feels futile to him since it only comes after he has lost the thing he cares most about. But the spirit Ariel sings a song to Alonso's son: "Full fathom five thy father lies; Of his bones are coral made; Those are pearls that were his eyes; Nothing of him that doth fade But doth suffer a sea change Into something rich and strange".

Alonso's grief is aroused by an illusion, an imitation of an action, but his repentance is real, and is slowly transforming him into a different man. Who is this new man? Let us take counsel from the "honest old councilor" Gonzalo, who always has the clearest sight in the play. He tells us that on this voyage, when so much seemed lost, every traveller found *himself* "When no man was his own". The something rich and strange into which Alonso changes is himself, as he was before his life took a wrong turn. Prospero's magic does no more than arrest people in a potent illusion; in his power they are "knit up In their distractions". When released, he says, "they shall be themselves".

On virtually every page of the *Tempest*, the word *wonder* appears, or else some synonym for it. Miranda's name is Latin for wonder, her favourite adjective brave seems to mean both good and out-of-the-ordinary, and the combination rich *and strange* means the same. What is wonder? J. V. Cunningham describes it in the book I mentioned as the shocked limit of all feeling, in which fear, sorrow, and joy can all merge. There is some truth in that, but it misses what is wonderful or wondrous about wonder. It suggests that in wonder our feelings are numbed and we are left limp, wrung dry of all emotion. But wonder is itself a feeling, the one to which Miranda is always giving voice, the powerful sense that what is before one is both strange and good. Wonder does not numb the other feelings; what it does is dislodge them from their habitual moorings.

The experience of wonder is the disclosure of a sight or thought or image that fits no habitual context of feeling or understanding, but grabs and holds us by a power borrowed from nothing apart from itself. The two things that Plotinus says characterize beauty, that the soul recognizes it at first glance and spontaneously gives welcome to it, equally describe the experience of wonder. The beautiful always produces wonder, if it is seen as beautiful, and the sense of wonder always sees beauty.

But are there really no wonders that are ugly? The monstrosities that used to be exhibited in circus side-shows are wonders too, are they not? In the *Tempest*, three characters think first of all of such spectacles when they lay eyes on Caliban, but they are incapable of wonder, since they think they know everything that matters already. A fourth character in the same batch, who is drunk but not insensible, gives way at the end of Act II to the sense that this is not just someone strange and deformed, nor just a useful servant, but a brave monster. But Stephano is not like the holiday fools who pay to see monstrosities like two-headed calves or exotic sights like wild men of Borneo. I recall an aquarium somewhere in Europe that had on display an astoundingly ugly catfish. People came casually up to its tank, were startled, made noises of disgust, and turned away. Even to be arrested before such a sight feels in some way perverse and has some conflict in the feeling it arouses, as when we stare at the victims of a car wreck. The sight of the ugly or disgusting, when it is felt as such, does not have the settled repose or willing surrender that are characteristic of wonder. "Wonder is sweet," as Aristotle says.

This sweet contemplation of something outside us is exactly opposite to Alonso's painful immersion in his own remorse, but in every other respect he is a model of the spectator of a tragedy. We are in the power of another for awhile, the sight of an illusion works real and durable changes in us, we merge into something rich and strange, and what we find by being absorbed in the image of another is ourselves. As Alonso is shown a mirror of his soul by Prospero, we are shown a mirror of ourselves in Alonso, but in that mirror we see ourselves as we are not in witnessing the *Tempest,* but in witnessing.a tragedy.

The *Tempest* is a beautiful play, suffused with wonder as well as with reflections on wonder, but it holds the intensity of the tragic experience at a distance. Homer, on the other hand, has pulled off a feat even more astounding than Shakespeare's, by imitating the experience of a spectator of tragedy within a story that itself works on us as a tragedy.

In Book XXIV of the Iliad, forms of the word *tham bos,* amazement, occur three times in three lines, when Priam suddenly appears in the hut of Achilles and "kisses the terrible man-slaughtering hands that killed his many sons", but this is only the prelude to the true wonder. Achilles and Priam cry together, each for his own grief, as each has cried so often before, but this time a miracle happens. Achilles' grief is transformed into satisfaction, and cleansed from his chest and his hands.

This is all the more remarkable, since Achilles has for days been repeatedly trying to take out his raging grief on Hector's dead body. The famous first word of the *Iliad, mÍnis,* wrath, has come back at the beginning of Book XXIV in the participle *meneainôn* , a constant condition that Lattimore translates well as "standing fury."

But all this hardened rage evaporates in one lamentation, just because Achilles shares it with his enemy's father. Hermes had told Priam to appeal to Achilles in the names of his father, his mother, and his child, "in order to stir his heart", but Priam's focussed misery goes straight to Achilles' heart without diluting the effect.

The first words out of Priam's mouth are "remember your father". Your father deserves pity, Priam says, so "pity me with him in mind, since I am more pitiful even than he; I have dared what no other mortal on earth ever dared, to stretch out my lips to the hand of the man who murdered my children".

Achilles had been pitying Patroclus, but mainly himself, but the feeling to which Priam has directed him now is exactly the same as tragic pity. Achilles is looking at a human being who has chosen to go to the limits of what is humanly possible to search for something that matters to him.

The wonder of this sight takes Achilles out of his self-pity, but back into himself as a son and as a sharer of human misery itself. All his old longings for glory and revenge fall away, since they have no place in the sight in which he is now absorbed. For the moment, the beauty of Priam's terrible action re-makes the world, and determines what matters and what doesn't.

The feeling in this moment out of time is fragile, and Achilles feels it threatened by tragic fear. In the strange fusion of this scene, what Achilles fears is himself; "don't irritate me any longer now, old man," he says when Priam tries to hurry along the return of Hector's body, "don't stir up my heart in its griefs any more now, lest I not spare even you yourself'.

Finally, after they share a meal, they just look at each other. "Priam wondered at Achilles, at how big he was and what he was like, for he seemed equal to the gods, but Achilles wondered at Trojan Priam, looking on the worthy sight of him and hearing his story". In the grip of wonder they do not see enemies. They see truly. They see the beauty in two men who have lost almost everything. They see a son a father should be proud of and a father a son should revere.

The action of the *Iliad* stretches from Achilles' deliberate choice to remove himself from the war to his deliberate choice to return Hector's body to Priam. The passion of the *Iliad* moves from anger through pity and fear to wonder. Priam's wonder lifts him for a moment out of the misery he is enduring, and permits him to see the cause of that misery as still something good. Achilles' wonder is similar to that of Priam, since Achilles too sees the cause of his anguish in a new light, but in his case this takes several steps. When Priam first appears in his hut, Homer compares the amazement this produces to that with which people look at a murderer who has fled from his homeland.

This is a strange comparison, and it recalls the even stranger fact disclosed one book earlier that Patroclus, whom everyone speaks of as gentle and kind-hearted, who gives his life because he cannot bear to see his friends destroyed to satisfy Achilles' anger, this same Patroclus began his life as a murderer in his own country, and came to Achilles' father Peleus for a second chance at life.

When Achilles remembers his father, he is remembering the man whose kindness brought Patroclus into his life, so that his tears, now for his father, now again for Patroclus, merge into a single grief. But the old man crying with him is a father too, and Achilles' tears encompass Priam along with Achilles' own loved ones. Finally, since Priam is crying for Hector, Achilles' grief includes Hector himself, and so it turns his earlier anguish inside out. If Priam is like Achilles' father, then Hector must come to seem to Achilles to be like a brother, or to be like himself.

Achilles cannot be brought to such a reflection by reasoning, nor do the feelings in which he has been embroiled take him in that direction. Only Priam succeeds in unlocking Achilles' heart, and he does so by an action, by kissing his hand. From the beginning of Book XVIII (23, 27, 33), Achilles' hands are referred to over and over and over, as he uses them to pour dirt on his head, to tear his hair, and to kill every Trojan he can get his hands on.

Hector, who must go up against those hands, is mesmerized by them; they are like a fire, he says, and repeats it. "His hands seem like a fire" (XX, 371-2). After Priam kisses Achilles' hand, and after they cry together, Homer tells us that the desire for lamentation went out of Achilles' chest and out of his hands (XXIV, 514).

His murderous, manslaughtering hands are stilled by a grief that finally has no enemy to take itself out on. When, in Book XVIII, Achilles had accepted his doom , it was part of a bargain; "I will lie still when I am dead," he had said, "but now I must win splendid glory" . But at the end of the poem, Achilles has lost interest in glory. He is no longer eaten up by the desire to be lifted above Hector and Priam, but comes to rest in just looking at them for what they are. Homer does surround Achilles in armor that takes the sting from his misery and from his approaching death, by working that misery and death into the wholeness of the Iliad. But the *Iliad* is, as Aristotle says, the prototype of tragedy; it is not a poem that aims at conferring glory but a poem that bestows the gift of wonder. Like Alonso in the Tempest, Achilles ultimately finds himself. Of the two, Achilles is the closer model of the spectator of a tragedy, because Alonso plunges deep into remorse before he is brought back into the shared world. Achilles is lifted directly out of himself, into the shared world, in the act of wonder, and sees his own image in the sorrowing father in front of him. This is exactly what a tragedy does to us, and exactly what we experience in looking at Achilles. In his loss, we pity him. In his fear of himself, on Priam's behalf, we fear for him, that he might lose his new-won humanity. In his capacity to be moved by the wonder of a suffering fellow human, we wonder at him.

At the end of the Iliad, as at the end of every tragedy, we are washed in the beauty of the human image, which our pity and our fear have brought to sight. The five marks of tragedy that we learned of from Aristotle's *Poetics*—that it imitates an action, arouses pity and fear, displays the human image as such, ends in wonder, and is inherently beautiful—give a true and powerful account of the tragic pleasure.

Excerpts from Aristotle's Poetics

Ch. 6 A tragedy is an imitation of an action that is serious and has a wholeness in its extent, in language that is pleasing (though in distinct ways in its different parts), enacted rather than narrated, culminating, by means of pity and fear, in the cleansing of these passions...So tragedy is an imitation not of people, but of action, life, and happiness or unhappiness, while happiness and unhappiness have their being in activity, and come to completion not in a quality but in some sort of action...Therefore it is deeds and the story that are the end at which tragedy aims, and in all things the end is what matters most...So the source that governs tragedy in the way that the soul governs life is the story.

Ch. 7 An extended whole is that which has a beginning, middle and end. But a beginning is something which, in itself, does not need to be after anything else, while something else naturally is the case or comes about after it; and an end is its contrary, something which in itself is of such a nature as to be after something else, either necessarily or for the most part, but to have nothing else after it-It is therefore needful that wellput-together stories not begin from just anywhere at random, nor end just anywhere at random...And beauty resides in size and order...the oneness and wholeness of the beautiful thing being present all at once in contemplation...in stories, just as in human organizations and in living things.

Ch. 8 A story is not one, as some people think, just because it is about one person...And Homer, just as he is distinguished in all other ways, seems to have seen this point beautifully, whether by art or by nature.

Ch. 9 Now tragedy is an imitation not only of a complete action, but also of objects of fear and pity, and these arise most of all when events happen contrary to expectation but in consequence of one another; for in this way they will have more wonder in them than if they happened by chance or by fortune, since even among things that happen by chance, the greatest sense of wonder is from those that seem to have happened by design.

Chs. 13-14 Since it is peculiar to tragedy to be an imitation of actions arousing pity and fear...and since the former concerns someone who is undeserving of suffering and the latter concerns someone like us...the story that works well must...depict a change from good to bad fortune, resulting not from badness one that arises from the actions themselves, the astonishment coming about through things that are likely, as in the Oedipus of Sophocles. A revelation, as the word indicates, is a change from ignorance to knowledge, that produces either friendship or hatred in people marked out for good or bad fortune. The most beautiful of revelations occurs when reversals of condition come about at the same time, as is the case in the Oedipus.—Ch. 11

Chs. 24-5 Wonder needs to be produced in tragedies, but in the epic there is more room for that which confounds reason, by means of which wonder comes about most of all, since in the epic one does not see the person who performs the action; the events surrounding the pursuit of Hector would seem ridiculous if they were on stage...But wonder is sweet...And Homer most of all has taught the rest of us how one ought to speak of what is untrue...One ought to choose likely impossibilities in preference to unconvincing possibilities...And if a poet has, represented impossible things, then he has missed the mark, but that is the right thing to do if he thereby hits the mark that is the end of the poetic art itself, that is, if in that way he makes that or some other part more wondrous.

Chapter 6

Complexity and Pleasure: Aristotle's 'Complex Plot' and the Pleasure Element in Tragedy

In his Poetics Aristotle (384-322 BC) classifies plot into two types: simple [haplos], and complex [peplegmenos]. The simple plot is defined as a unified construct of necessary and probable actions accompanied by a change of fortune. The complex plot, says Aristotle, is accompanied by two other features, namely; peripeteia or reversal, and anagnorisis, or recognition. It is this which Aristotle feels is the best kind of tragic plot, in that it provides the best possibility of delivering tragic pleasure.

Before we look at the distinctive features of the complex plot, it would perhaps be instructive to examine those features which it shares with the simple plot. The unity of structure recommended by Aristotle includes the tripartite division of the plot into the beginning, the middle and the end, as well as the unities of time and action. He stresses unified action, where all action in the plot carries a definite link to other actions, and subsequent actions are the necessary and probable outcomes of the former.

Necessary and probable are terms which recur throughout the Poetics. They stand for the universality of poetry in that they point to how or what actions should logically be in a given situation. Unity of action, therefore, does not mean all that happens to the protagonist, but precisely what comprises a particular whole action according to the norms of necessity and probability. Unity of time, in contrast to its neo-classical applications, here simply means the time span in which the tragic action can be best comprehended by the audience, given the constraints of human memory, and the wholeness of the action.

Finally, we come to the change of fortune. It is either from good to bad or the reverse. The former is more characteristic of tragedy but in a later section Aristotle complicates the idea by saying that those plots where the catastrophe is averted by recognition are best. The change of fortune is also accompanied by a complication of events [desis] and their resolution [lusis].

Having briefly examined the common aspects of both kinds of plot, we can now look at the special attributes of the complex plot.

Let us take another look at Aristotle's celebrated definition of complex action: 'A complex action is one where the change is accompanied by such reversal or recognition or both.' Peripeteia has been defined as a reversal of the action. If, however, it is just that, then how is it different from the change of fortune? Clearly this is too limited a definition of peripeteia and it would perhaps be pertinent to consider two other definitions. Humphrey House defines it as a 'reversal of intention'. This definition takes into account the 'thought' or the dianoia exercised by the character. House describes it as 'holding the wrong end of the stick'. Peripeteia is therefore the turning of the stick thinking that it is the right end. The ignorance behind any peripeteia is not mere ignorance. It is the ignorance arising out of error.

The other definition is more recent. Frank Kermode defines it as a 'disconfirmation followed by a consonance; the interest of having our expectations falsified is obviously related to our wish to reach discovery by an unexpected route. It has nothing to do with our reluctance to get there at all. So that in assimilating the peripeteia we are enacting that readjustment of our expectations in regard to an end'. This points out the pleasure we receive from peripeteia which is quite different from the straightforward following of a narrative to its end, or in other words, mere change of fortune.

Having defined peripeteia and identified its characteristic pleasure, we must also consider what this pleasure actually consists of. This is the element of surprise or wonder [Gk. Thaumaston]. The source of wonder is often the tragic recognition or anagnorisis. Recognition has been variously defined. In Aristotle it is the recognition of persons through tokens, artistic contrivances, memory, reasoning (including false inferences) and lastly, arising out of the events themselves (as in Oedipus Rex).

Aristotle defines this anagnorisis as a change from ignorance to knowledge. In terms of Humphrey House's analogy, it would mean the realization that you have got hold of the wrong end of the stick. House himself defines recognition thus, 'The discovery of the truth of the matter is the ghastly wakening from the state of the ignorance which is the very essence of hamartia.' Other scholars define it variously as 'a way in which the emotional potential... can be brought to its highest voltage, so to speak at the moment of discharge', or, 'recognition brings its illumination, which can shed retrospective light'.

Aristotle likes best the recognition which arises out of the events themselves, as in Sophocles's Oedipus Rex. The whole play is a step by step unraveling of Oedipus's true identity and Oedipus's holding the wrong end of the stick, as it were, in trying to discover his identity without knowing that the results will be catastrophic. At second best, he places those tragedies where reasoning affects the recognition. Together with these definitions, we could compare the slightly different angle from which Terence Cave views recognition. For him it is a stumbling block to belief which disturbs the decorum. From this comparison we realise the complicated nature of recognition.

In the unravelling of the complex plot the point of the recognition is very different from that possible in a simple plot. The combination of peripeteia and recognition does not merely affect the characters in the tragedy. They can also extend to the audience or the reader. The unexpectedness of the tragic catastrophe which the complex plot brings [the element of wonder or thaumaston heightens our feelings of pity and fear as well as other related emotions.

Here it would be useful to look at another famous assertion of Aristotle's. In Ch XIV of the Poetics he says, 'the pleasure which the poet should afford is that which comes from pity and fear through imitation'. Perhaps an examination of pity and fear together with imitation can give us a better idea of the pleasures incidental to tragedy. Let us start with an appraisal of pity and fear. Pity and fear are man's sympathy for the good part of mankind in the bad part of their experiences.

Pity is evoked when there is a discrepancy between the agent and Fate, and fear when there is a likeness between the agent and us. Stephen Dedalus defines Pity and Fear in James Joyce's A Portrait of the Artist as a Young Man. He calls pity the feeling which arrests the mind in the presence of whatsoever is grave and constant in human-sufferings and unites it with the human sufferer. Terror, or fear, is that which unites it with the secret cause.

Aristotle himself gives similar definitions of these terms in his Rhetoric [books V and II]. There he defines them as a species of pain. It is here that we can begin to consider the idea that tragic pleasure derives from the purgation of these emotions. The idea of purgation as a medical metaphor has been in vogue for a long time and can be substantiated by examples from Aristotle's Problems [problem XXX] where coldness of black bile accompanies 'despair and fear' and heat is the suggested cure which restores the temperature to a temperate mean. Aristotle, unlike his teacher Plato, says that the emotions are good in themselves.

Therefore there should be no need to purge the feelings of pity and fear. Instead, a more sensible definition of tragic pleasure would be that concomitant with the proper feeling of these emotions. By proper I mean a temperate attitude to these emotions as Aristotle teaches in his Nichomachean Ethics. In Book II of his Ethics, he says: fear and confidence and appetite and anger and pity and in general pleasure and pain may be felt both too much and too little, and in both cases not well; but to feel them at the right times, with reference to the right objects, towards the right people, with the right motive, and in the right way, is what is both intermediate and best, and this is characteristic of virtue.

Aristotle's idea of the mean is derived from the Pythagoreans who applied it to music. Here we may note that another place where Aristotle uses the term catharsis is in his Politics and in the context of giving 'relief to overcharged feeling' through music. Interestingly, here too, he mentions pity and fear among the emotions dealt with and the restoration is once again to a temperate mean.

Is catharsis the only possible source of pleasure in tragedy? Humphry House does not think so. Those who are temperate in themselves and do not require an adjustment of their emotional reactions to tragic situations, still derive pleasure from tragedy.

Even Plato in The Republic testifies to this fact: 'even the best of us enjoy it and let ourselves be carried away by our feelings; and are full of praises for the merits of the poet who can most powerfully affect us in this way.'. The pleasure arising out of poetry is therefore not entirely dependent on catharsis. Instead, it works in two ways. In Book VII [section 11 - 14] Aristotle discusses 'pure' pleasure and 'incidental' pleasure. The former is universal and is accompanied by no pain and is likened to the pleasure arising out of contemplation. Those who experience this do so solely by contemplating and appraising the imitation of human emotions in tragedy.

It is through this view that we bring our focus back on the last part of Aristotle's statement quoted above. Pleasure is effected through imitation [or mimesis]. As Aristotle said imitation is itself a pleasurable act. All of this applies to epic as well as tragedy and can probably be extended to other types of poetry. The specifically 'tragic' pleasure is that pertaining to the medium and the dramatic mode of tragedy. These constitute the specific imitative aspects of tragedy.

The idea of tragic pleasure therefore necessarily consists as Aristotle aptly puts it 'in that which comes with pity and fear through imitation'. A heightened sense of pity and fear is effected when the necessary and probable events take an unexpected turn. This is possible in the complex plot with the accompanying peripeteia and anagnorisis. Thus our examination of the elements of the complex plot has led us to a consideration of pity and fear. These together with imitation [or mimesis] help us understand the pleasure peculiar to tragedy.

Chapter 7

Some Aristotelian Principles

Genre and Generic Attributes

Aristotle sought to anchor his definitions of literary genres in exemplary works and authors. Of tragedians, he considered Sophocles the best, and his Oedipus Tyrannus ("Oedipus the King") the finest example. That's immediately debatable because great works by two other major tragedians survived (Aeschylus and Euripides). In the case of epics, his task was easier because only one author's work were widely known to him, those of Homer. According to Aristotle, the lost Homeric mock battle narrative, Margites, is to comic drama as the Iliad and the Odyssey are to tragedy. Note that this suggests genres originate in pairs, each balancing qualities the other excells in with qualities it lacks and its partner has in abundance.

When distinguishing between epic and tragedy, he said epic has a multiplicity of plots, each of which is fully developed in the epic's larger scope, but the tragedy is a compressed development of a single plot. Aristotle says epics have a major advantage over tragedy because of their multiplicity of incident, the capacity to enlarge its action to incorporate several series of events which may have happened simultaneously [representing them in narrative series by means of flashbacks, etc.].

Mimesis/Imitation

For Aristotle, all literature is an art of imitation (Gk. *mimesis,* whence "mime"). As artists imitated life to produce their literature, audiences would be inspired to imitate, in some fashion, what they read, heard or saw on the stage. The social function of epic as an exemplar of good behaviour was easier for Aristotle to assume in Classical Greece. Recently, the hero-aesthetic has been dethroned as a necessary and great model of human aspiration, at least as it motivates citizens to become warriors. Comedy produced an immediate problem for Aristotle, however, since comedies tend to be about bad behaviour and people doing ugly, immoral, or ridiculous things. He accepted that the primary object of comedy as imitation: imitation of low characters—not morally bad, but ludicrous, ugly but not painful or destructive. He defended comedies mimetic representation of ludicrous behaviour because it would incite audiences to avoid its imitation.

Proper Proportion

A tragedy imitates action that is serious, complete, and of an appropriate magnitude (neither trivial nor too vast).

Literature's Function

The tragedy evokes two kinds of emotions, pity and fear, in order to cleanse the mind of dangerous but natural human tendencies, especially overgrown pride in our accomplishments. This emotional purging (*katharsis*), when shared by the whole population, restored the city to health.

Character Construction

Tragic characters all have two qualities by which we judge them: thought and character. In order of importance, proper characters should have the following qualities: goodness in a moral sense, appropriateness to social mores, truth to life (probability in small details), and consistency (i.e., not disturbingly divided in nature).

Sub-components of Dramatic Theater

Tragedies have these six parts: plot, character, diction, thought, spectacle (today, "special effects"), and song.

Literature and human nature

According to Aristotle, our qualities are determined by

our characters, those basic combinations of traits we were born with or develop as we grow, but we are made happy or wretched by our actions. Therefore, the great literature concentrates on showing us those actions at crucial moments and the "first principle" of any drama is its plot (i.e., the action). A perfect tragedy should imitate complex actions (see #12) that excite pity and fear while leading a man who is extraordinarily good and just to misfortune by some error of judgment or frailty of character. That "frailty of character" is the famous "tragic flaw" or *hamartia,* actually something closer to a "tragic imbalance"

Completeness of a Work of Literature ("Unities of form and Time")

The key qualities in the construction of a tragedy's plot are: it has a beginning, middle, and end (i.e., is complete); and it is of appropriate size to be "easily embraced in one view" or "easily embraced by the memory" [long enough to move a character "from calamity to good fortune, or from good fortune to calamity." For this reason, Aristotle says good plays resemble living organisms. (This idea has a rebirth in Romanticism's "organic form" theory.) An "episodic" plot is: one that moves from incident to incident without necessary or probable cause. You can still find modern literary reviews that condemn a work's plot as "episodic," though since Modernism, fiction has tended to test that boundary and many of the rest Aristotle tried to establish.

"Unity of Action"

In addition to unity of form and time, Aristotle also said a plot should be unified. However, definitions of this tend to be circular: the plot centers around an action that is unified.

Poetry vs. History—the "Truth" Problem

The ancients and medieval theorists were troubled that poetic works of all kinds (narrative fiction, drama, lyrics) are technically lies. isn't lying a bad thing, something to be punished. Aristotle saw the poet and historian as his opposing binary opposites to solve this problem. The poet's job differs from the historian's in that: the historian must relate what happened, but the poet may relate what may (or may have) happened.

Simple vs. Complex Plots

While Aristotle tended to favor literary traits that unified, he was not against complexity, itself. For him, a complex plot is distinguished from a simple one because it has one or both of these special features which produce important effects in the audience: reversal of expectations ("peripeteia") and/or recognition (usually of someone's identity, often of one's own true identity ["anagnorisis"]). Both of these events occur nearly simultaneously near the end of Oedipus Tyrannus. Aristotelian analysis divides the play's action into two parts complication and unraveling, the latter of which might begin with the reversal of expectations and end with the self-discovery or recognition scene.

Literature and the "Agon"

Like most Classical Greeks, Aristotle saw most of the universe as a pattern of struggle, or "*agon*," in which opposed forces battled for supremacy. Tragedy and epic, alike, according to Aristotle, might develop a kind of collision between opposing character types in which one must subdue the other. He said tragedy should have a "double thread," which can be identified by: its concern for two groups of actors whose ends are opposite because of their opposite natures (e.g., in epic, Odysseus' triumphant return vs the suitors' destruction; in tragedy, Antigone's unwavering insistence on the old burial customs' vs. Creon's equally stubborn demand that she obey the city's law as he has articulated it).

Spectacle/Special Effects vs. Tragic or Comic Effects

Aristotle distinguished clearly between works which operated upon the audience's minds by manipulating the emotions via thoughtful processes from those which sought their impact by shocking the audience with scenes which were taboo in ordinary social life (e.g., murders, open sexuality, violent accidents). The movies, Halloween and Nightmare on Elm Street, and all their many imitators, are examples of tragedies that use spectacle to move the audience's emotions. An alternative means of moving the audience's emotions is having painful circumstances strike those who are either friends or related to each other.

Tradition and the Individual Talent

T.S. Eliot's essay by that name, describes the process by which great art derives from the teachings and examples of previous eras' greatest works. However, this raises the question of how much change can be made in plots or characters or situations borrowed from previous works. For the Greeks, the problem was religious, since the mythic stories of the gods and heroes which were adapted by the playwrights were still part of functioning Greek religion in the Classical era. Aristotle says there is one restriction on the poet's adaptation of legends: "he may not destroy the framework of the received legends." Obviously, this raises the same "essentialist" question we see in other Aristotelian principles of interpretation and creation. Who can say what the "framework" is and what is non-essential? Did Helen go to Troy, or did the Trojans and Greeks fight over a phantom sent by the gods to destroy them? Can that kind of question be raised by a work of literature, or does that somehow violate the "rules"?

Poetry, Inspiration and Madness

Unlike Plato, whose "Ion" attempts to prove poets are out of their minds when they compose, Aristotle allowed more room for the poet's witting craft to produce literature. However, Aristotle believes really great poets must be either specially gifted (able to imitate any kind of human character) or mad (unable to maintain their own characters).

Chapter 8

Aristotle's Poetics: A New Approach to Catharsis

We have always had a literary or possibly medical view of catharsis in the Poetics, one way or another. I would like to try another direction:

- I am convinced that the Socratic elenchus is based on a mathematical model. First something is proved to be equal to something else, then another thing is proved to be equal to the same "something else". Since the first and second things are not the same (by definition) the argument cancels itself, and we are left with aporia. This has always been taken as a philosophical statement, but since mathematics are in Greek terms philosophical in nature, I read the elenchus as a direct anticipation of what Euclid was later to codify as "Things equal to the same thing are equal to each other" and if not equal to each other, the process is wrong. Used for self-clarification, the mathematical base is apparent, to be found in the axiom to Bk I of Euclid. [If a = b, and b = c, then a = c, but if in the real world it does not, we goofed in our thinking. Socrates is exploring philosophical goofs, a good thing to do for a philosopher!.
- Catharsis can be seen as a mathematical process of cancellation, if it operates on two factors which are inherently inverses of each other. If eleos and t can be seen as inverse emotional states, which is hard to

> do since we do not have an authentic Greek psychological discipline, then the "processing" of these two together, at the same time while watching the same dramatic sequence, should reveal a "null". In short, if I am computing (+x + -x) I get O. Now the problem would be this: Are pity and fear inverses? I believe they are, eleos being an outgoing emotion from the drama-watcher TOWARD a person of action, it has a positive (yang) quality, emptying the beholder's "heart" (Aristotle's wrong theory...). But deos is quite the opposite, it is a shrinking, in pulling emotion, which fills the "heart" with apprehension, sense of personal danger, risk. It sucks inward, yin-wise. If these two can be combined at a single time, the beholder may go out of the theater with a "null" or empty feeling.

I think this is often the feeling one gets after watching good modern Cinema, this null-ness, often almost numbness, which opens the mind to calmness, re-consideration, thoughtfulness. These are the qualities many of use feel after reading a Greek drama right- through. Mathematical patterns are often used by Plato for other than mathematical purposes.

A prime example of reaching a philosophical null, and then trying a new direction, is the puzzle in the middle of the Meno about triangles, which defies every mathematical solution, and leaves us with a "method of approximation", clearly intentionally. The rest of the Meno goes on to non-mathematical, mystical views seen through priestly eyes. Here is the beginning of a "farewell to mathematics", the turning point. And when we reach the Myth of Er, it will be shapes (topology) not mathematically calculable geometry, with which Plato has replaced his earlier faith in current mathematical developments to lead him to the higher reaches of pure thought.

Chapter 9

Character List

Aeschylus: Aeschylus is the author of the frequently-cited Oresteia, a play trilogy which includes Agamemnon. Aristotle attributes Aeschylus with a number of important innovations in the theater, including introducing a second actor, diminishing the importance of the chorus, and focusing on dialogue rather than music or dance (both of which were important elements in Ancient Greek theater). But Aristotle also faults Aeschylus, arguing that the playwright did not create a distinct poetic language.

Euripides: Aristotle refers to the tragedian Euripides - the author of Medea, The Bacchae, and over seventy other plays of which only nineteen have survived - as a master of plot. Aristotle comes to Euripides' defence often in the *Poetics*, saying that though critics censured his work as morose, his plays were often the best because they were the 'most tragic.' Aristotle conceives of the tragic effectin Euripedes' plays as flowing from the inner logic of their plots, which always included a fall from good fortune to bad.

Sophocles: Sophocles is the author of Oedipus, and considered by Aristotle the master of the tragedy. He draws men 'as they ought to be,' and creates a higher view of humans. Aristotle compares Sophocles to Homer for his tendency to idealize humanity. The playwright is also credited with raising the number of actors on the stage to three, and with adding scene-painting as a part of spectacle.

Chapter 10

Major Themes

Cathartic Reversal: Aristotle argues that the best tragedies - and thus the best plays, since Aristotle considers tragedy to be the highest dramatic form - use reversal and recognition to achieve catharsis. He writes that reversal works with a story's spine or centre to ensure that the hero comes full circle. Oedipus is his exemplar of a hero who undergoes such a reversal and thus has cathartic self-recognition. Aristotle considers catharsis to be a form of redemption. For instance, even though Oedipus' recognition is tragic it still redeems him: he is no longer living in ignorance of his tragedy but instead has accepted fate.

And redemption is not the only result of catharsis; the audience too undergoes a catharsis of sorts in a good drama. The hero's catharsis induces both pity and fear in the audience: pity for the hero, and fear that his fate could happen to us.

Complication and Denouement: There are only two parts to a good drama, says Aristotle - the rising action leading to the climax, which is known as the complication, and the denouement, or the 'unraveling' that follows the climax. This twofold movement follows Aristotle's theory of poetic unity. The complication leads up to the revelation of the unity at the heart of the work. After this revelation, a play naturally turns to the denouement, in which the significance and ramifications of the unity are explored and resolved.

The Imitative Nature of Art: There are two common ways to think of art: some consider it to be an expression of what is original and unusual in human thinking; Aristotle, on the other hand, argues that that art is 'imitative,' that is to say, representative of life. This imitative quality fascinates Aristotle. He devotes much of the *Poetics* to exploring the methods, significance, and consequences of this imitation of life. Aristotle concludes that art's imitative tendencies are expressed in one of three ways: a poet attempts to portray our world as it is, as we think it is, or as it ought to be.

The Standard of Poetic Judgment: Aristotle thinks that this tendency to criticize a work of art for factual errors - such as lack of historical accuracy - is misguided. He believes that instead we should a judge work according to its success at imitating the world. If the imitation is carried out with integrity and if the artwork's 'unity' is intact at its conclusion, a simple error in accuracy will do little to blemish this greater success. Art, in other words, should be judged aesthetically, not scientifically.

Tragedy vs. Epic Poetry: In Aristotle's time, the critics considered epic poetry to be the supreme art form, but to Aristotle, tragedy is the better of the two forms. Aristotle believes that tragedy, like the epic, can entertain and edify in its written form, but also has the added dimension of being able to translate onstage into a drama of spectacle and music, capable of being digested in one sitting.

Tragic Hero: The tragic hero, in Aristotle's view of drama, is not an eminently 'good' man; nor is he necessarily a paragon of virtue that is felled by adversity. Instead, the hero has some 'frailty' or flaw that is evident from the outset of a play that eventually ensures his doom. The audience, moreover, must be able to identify with this tragic flaw.

The Unity of Poetry: Aristotle often speaks of the unity of poetry in the *Poetics*; what he means by "unity," however, is sometimes misunderstood. Unity refers to the ability of the best dramatic plots to revolve around a central axis that 'unites' all the action. Aristotle believes that a unified drama will have a 'spine': a central idea which motivates all the action, character, thoughts, diction and spectacle in the play.

Chapter 11

Glossary of Terms

Catharsis: Catharsis is a key element of tragedy which induces pity and fear in the audience: pity of the hero's plight, and fear that it will befall us

Character: Character is one of the six components of tragedy that refers not to the 'attributes' of a given person, but the person himself as a representative entity in the play.

Comedy: Comedy presents human beings as "worse than they are" in life, in order to present a different type of imitation than in a classical tragedy.

Complex plot: A complex plot involves a unity of action and purpose and ultimately leads to a climactic reversal and recognition.

Complication: Complication is the rising action of a dramatic work that extends from the beginning of the play to the climax or reversal.

Denouement: Denouement is the unraveling of the plot that takes place after the climax.

Diction: Diction is one of the six components of tragedy; it includes how an actor delivers the lines written for him.

Drama: Drama presents actions before an audience with the use of actors, rather than oral recitation by a single narrator.

Epic: Epic presents actions through narrative and is usually recited orally by a single narrator.

Hexameter: Hexameter is the 'epic' meter or a line of 'six feet.'

Iambic: Iambic is the 'dramatic' meter with a syncopated beat, more closely related to the way we speak in normal life.

Imitation: Imitation is the defining purpose of all artists to represent life as it is, as we think it is, or as it should be.

Narrative: Narrative is the dramatization of action by a single narrator.

Pity: Pity is one of the key elements of catharisis, driven by our empathy for the hero's plight.

Plot: Plot is one of the six components of tragedy, but the most important. Aristotle calls plot the "soul of tragedy," since it is the arrangements of incidents that justifies all the other elements of tragedy in its dramatization of action.

Poetry: Poetry is any form of art which seeks to imitate life through words (or the rhythm of words).

Simple plot: A simple plot is a plot that doesn't necessarily maintain unity, reversal or recognition; can be episodic.

Song: A song is one form of conveying action in a tragedy.

Spectacle: Spectacle is one of the six components of tragedy; it includes anything that is presented before the audience onstage. Aristotle notes this is the least significant aspect of tragedy, since it is not vital to the actual 'text,' which can be read alone.

Thought: Thought is speech by characters used to explain, justify, or substitute for physical action.

Tragedy: Tragedy is an imitation of action that is serious, complete, of significant magnitude, depicted with rhythmic language and/or song, in the form of action (not narrative), that produces a 'purgation' of pity and fear in the audience.

Unity: Unity is the revolution of a work around a central axis, theme, or purpose. All components of the work must work towards this central purpose.

Chapter 12

Plot Overview

Aristotle proposes to discuss poetry, which he defines as a means of *mimesis*, or imitation, by means of language, rhythm, and harmony. As creatures who thrive on imitation, we are naturally drawn to poetry.

In particular, Aristotle focuses his discussion on tragedy, which uses dramatic, rather than narrative, form, and deals with agents who are better than us ourselves. Tragedy serves to arouse the emotions of pity and fear and to effect a *katharsis* (catharsis) of these emotions. Aristotle divides tragedy into six different parts, ranking them in order from most important to least important as follows: (1) *mythos*, or plot, (2) character, (3) thought, (4) diction, (5) melody, and (6) spectacle.

The first essential to creating a good tragedy is that it should maintain unity of plot. This means that the plot must move from beginning to end according to a tightly organized sequence of necessary or probable events. The beginning should not necessarily follow from any earlier events, and the end should tie up all loose ends and not produce any necessary consequences. The plot can also be enhanced by an intelligent use of *peripeteia*, or reversal, and *anagnorisis*, or recognition. These elements work best when they are made an integral part of the plot.

A plot should consist of a hero going from happiness to misery. The hero should be portrayed consistently and in a good light, though the poet should also remain true to what we know of the character. The misery should be the result of some *hamartia*, or error, on the part of the hero. A tragic plot must always involve some sort of tragic deed, which can be done or left undone, and this deed can be approached either with full knowledge or in ignorance. Aristotle discusses thought and diction and then moves on to address epic poetry. Epic poetry is similar to tragedy in many ways, though it is generally longer, more fantastic, and deals with a greater scope of action. After addressing some problems of criticism, Aristotle argues that tragedy is superior to epic poetry.

Chapter 13

Analytical Overview

Aristotle approaches poetry with the same scientific method with which he treats physics and biology. He begins by collecting and categorizing all the data available to him and then he draws certain conclusions and advances certain theses in accordance with his analysis. In the case of tragedy, this means he divides it into six parts, identifies plot as the most important part, and examines the different elements of plot and character that seem to characterize successful tragedies. He tentatively suggests that tragedy ultimately aims at the arousal of pity and fear and at the *katharsis* of these emotions. Then he begins to lay out certain theories as to what makes a good tragedy: it must focus on a certain type of hero who must follow a certain trajectory within a plot that is tightly unified, etc. Aristotle's conclusions, then, are based less on personal taste and more on an observation of what tends to produce the most powerful effects.

Aristotle's method raises the fundamental question of whether poetry can be studied in the same way as the natural sciences. Though there are some benefits to Aristotle's method, the ultimate answer seems to be "no." The scientific method relies on the assumption that there are certain regularities or laws that govern the behaviour of the phenomena being investigated. This method has been particularly successful in the physical sciences: Isaac Newton, for example, managed to reduce all mechanical behaviour to three simple laws. However, art does not seem to be governed by unchanging, unquestionable laws in the same way that nature is. Art often thrives and progresses by questioning the assumptions or laws that a previous generation has accepted. While Aristotle insisted on the primacy and unity of plot, Samuel Beckett has achieved fame as one of this century's greatest playwrights by constructing plays that arguably have no plot at all. Closer to Aristotle's time, Euripides often violated the Aristotelian principles of structure and balance in a conscious effort to depict a universe that is neither structured nor balanced. Not surprisingly, Aristotle seems to have preferred Sophocles to Euripides.

These remarks on Sophocles and Euripides bring us to another problem of interpreting Aristotle: we have a very limited stock of Greek tragedies against which to test Aristotle's theories. Aristotle could have been familiar with hundreds, or even thousands, of tragedies. All we have today are thirty-three plays by three tragedians. As a result, it is difficult to say to what extent most tragedies fit Aristotle's observations. Those that we have, however, often grossly violate Aristotle's requirement. The best example we have of an Aristotelian tragedy is *Oedipus Rex*, so it is no wonder that Aristotle makes such frequent reference to it in his examples.

Three points stand out as probably the most important in the *Poetics*: (1) the interpretation of poetry as *mimesis*, (2) the insistence on the primacy and unity of *mythos*, or plot, and (3) the view that tragedy serves to arouse the emotions of pity and fear and then to effect a *katharsis* of these emotions. (1) is discussed in the commentary on Chapters 1–3, (2)is discussed in the commentary on Chapter 6 and Chapters 7–9, and (3) is discussed in the commentary on Chapter 6 as well.

Chapter 14

Translated Text

In the tenth book of the Republic, when Plato has completed his final burning denunciation of Poetry, the false Siren, the imitator of things which themselves are shadows, the ally of all that is low and weak in the soul against that which is high and strong, who makes us feed the things we ought to starve and serve the things we ought to rule, he ends with a touch of compunction: 'We will give her champions, not poets themselves but poet-lovers, an opportunity to make her defence in plain prose and show that she is not only sweet—as we well know—but also helpful to society and the life of man, and we will listen in a kindly spirit. For we shall be gainers, I take it, if this can be proved.' Aristotle certainly knew the passage, and it looks as if his treatise on poetry was an answer to Plato's challenge.

Few of the great works of ancient Greek literature are easy reading. They nearly all need study and comment, and at times help from a good teacher, before they yield up their secret. And the Poetics cannot be accounted an exception. For one thing the treatise is fragmentary. It originally consisted of two books, one dealing with Tragedy and Epic, the other with Comedy and other subjects. We possess only the first. For another, even the book we have seems to be unrevised and unfinished. The style, though luminous, vivid, and in its broader division systematic, is not that of a book intended for publication.

Like most of Aristotle's extant writing, it suggests the MS. of an experienced lecturer, full of jottings and adscripts, with occasional phrases written carefully out, but never revised as a whole for the general reader. Even to accomplished scholars the meaning is often obscure, as may be seen by a comparison of the three editions recently published in England, all the work of savants of the first eminence, or, still more strikingly, by a study of the long series of misunderstandings and overstatements and corrections which form the history of the Poetics since the Renaissance.

Pro f. Butcher, 1895 and 1898; Prof. Bywater, 1909; and Prof. Margoliouth, 1911. But it is of another cause of misunderstanding that I wish principally to speak in this preface. The great edition from which the present translation is taken was the fruit of prolonged study by one of the greatest Aristotelians of the nineteenth century, and is itself a classic among works of scholarship. In the hands of a student who knows even a little Greek, the translation, backed by the commentary, may lead deep into the mind of Aristotle. But when the translation is used, as it doubtless will be, by readers who are quite without the clue provided by a knowledge of the general habits of the Greek language, there must arise a number of new difficulties or misconceptions. To understand a great foreign book by means of a translation is possible enough where the two languages concerned operate with a common stock of ideas, and belong to the same period of civilization.

But between ancient Greece and modern England there yawn immense gulfs of human history; the establishment and the partial failure of a common European religion, the barbarian invasions, the feudal system, the regrouping of modern Europe, the age of mechanical invention, and the industrial revolution. In an average page of French or German philosophy nearly all the nouns can be translated directly into exact equivalents in English; but in Greek that is not so. Scarcely one in ten of the nouns on the first few pages of the Poetics has an exact English equivalent. Every proposition has to be reduced to its lowest terms of thought and then re-built.

This is a difficulty which no translation can quite deal with; it must be left to a teacher who knows Greek. And there is a kindred difficulty which flows from it. Where words can be translated into equivalent words, the style of an original can be closely followed; but no translation which aims at being written in normal English can reproduce the style of Aristotle. I have sometimes played with the idea that a ruthlessly literal translation, helped out by bold punctuation, might be the best. For instance, premising that the words poesis, poetes mean originally 'making' and 'maker', one might translate the first paragraph of the Poetics thus:— MAKING: kinds of making: function of each, and how the Myths ought to be put together if the Making is to go right.

Number of parts: nature of parts: rest of same inquiry.

Begin in order of nature from first principles.

Epos-making, tragedy-making (also comedy), dithyramb-making (and most fluting and harping), taken as a whole, are really not Makings but Imitations. They differ in three points; they imitate (a) different objects, (b) by different means, (c) differently (i.e. different manner).

Some artists imitate (i.e. depict) by shapes and colours. (Obs. sometimes by art, sometimes by habit.) Some by voice. Similarly the above arts all imitate by rhythm, language, and tune, and these either (1) separate or (2) mixed.

Rhythm and tune alone, harping, fluting, and other arts with same effect—e.g. panpipes. Rhythm without tune: dancing. (Dancers imitate characters, emotions, and experiences by means of rhythms expressed in form.) Language alone (whether prose or verse, and one form of verse or many): this art has no name up to the present (i.e. there is no name to cover mimes and dialogues and any similar imitation made in iambics, elegiacs, &c. Commonly people attach the 'making' to the meter and say 'elegiac-makers', 'hexameter-makers,' giving them a common class-name by their meter, as if it was not their imitation that makes them 'makers'). Such an experiment would doubtless be a little absurd, but it would give an English reader some help in understanding both Aristotle's style and his meaning.

For example, there i.e.lightenment in the literal phrase, 'how the myths ought to be put together.' The higher Greek poetry did not make up fictitious plots; its business was to express the heroic saga, the myths. Again, the literal translation of poetes, poet, as 'maker', helps to explain a term that otherwise seems a puzzle in the Poetics. If we wonder why Aristotle, and Plato before him, should lay such stress on the theory that art is imitation, it is a help to realise that common language called it 'making', and it was clearly not 'making' in the ordinary sense. The poet who was 'maker' of a Fall of Troy clearly did not make the real Fall of Troy. He made an imitation Fall of Troy. An artist who 'painted Pericles' really 'made an imitation Pericles by means of shapes and colours'. Hence we get started upon a theory of art which, whether finally satisfactory or not, is of immense importance, and are saved from the error of complaining that Aristotle did not understand the 'creative power' of art.

As a rule, no doubt, the difficulty, even though merely verbal, lies beyond the reach of so simple a tool as literal translation. To say that tragedy 'imitate god men' while comedy 'imitates bad men' strikes a modern reader as almost meaningless. The truth is that neither 'good' nor 'bad' is an exact equivalent of the Greek. It would be nearer perhaps to say that, relatively speaking, you look up to the characters of tragedy, and down upon those of comedy. High or low, serious or trivial, many other pairs of words would have to be called in, in order to cover the wide range of the common Greek words. And the point is important, because we have to consider whether in Chapter VI Aristotle really lays it down that tragedy, so far from being the story of un-happiness that we think it, is properly an imitation of eudaimonia—a word often translated 'happiness', but meaning something more like 'high life' or 'blessedness'.By water, with most editors, emends the text.

Another difficult word which constantly recurs in the Poetics is prattein or praxis, generally translated 'to act' or 'action'. But prattein, like our 'do', also has an intransitive meaning 'to fare' either well or ill; and Professor Margoliouth has pointed out that it seems more true to say that tragedy shows how men 'fare' than how they 'act'. It shows the experiences or fortunes rather than merely their deeds. But one must not draw the line too bluntly. I should doubt whether a classical Greek writer was ordinarily conscious of the distinction between the two meanings. Certainly it is easier to regard happiness as a way of faring than as a form of action. Yet Aristotle can use the passive of prattein for things 'done' or 'gone through'.

The fact is that much misunderstanding is often caused by our modern attempts to limit too strictly the meaning of a Greek word. Greek was very much a live language, and a language still unconscious of grammar, not, like ours, dominated by definitions and trained upon dictionaries. An instance is provided by Aristotle's famous saying that the typical tragic hero is one who falls from high state or fame, not through vice or depravity, but by some great hamartia. Hamartia means originally a 'bad shot' or 'error', but is currently used for 'offence' or 'sin'. Aristotle clearly means that the typical hero is a great man with 'something wrong' in his life or character; but I think it is a mistake of method to argue whether he means 'an intellectual error' or 'a moral flaw'. The word is not so precise.

Similarly, when Aristotle says that a deed of strife or disaster is more tragic when it occurs 'amid affections' or 'among people who love each other', no doubt the phrase, as Aristotle's own examples show, would primarily suggest to a Greek feuds between near relations. Yet some of the meaning is lost if one translates simply 'within the family'.

There is another series of obscurities or confusions in the Poetics which, unless I am mistaken, arises from the fact that Aristotle was writing at a time when the great age of Greek tragedy was long past, and was using language formed in previous generations. The words and phrases remained in the tradition, but the forms of art and activity which they denoted had sometimes changed in the interval. If we date the Poetics about the year 330 B.C., as seems probable, that is more than two hundred years after the first tragedy of Thespis was produced in Athens, and more than seventy after the death of the last great masters of the tragic stage. When we remember that a training in music and poetry formed a prominent part of the education of every wellborn Athenian, we cannot be surprised at finding in Aristotle, and to a less extent in Plato, considerable traces of a tradition of technical language and even of aesthetic theory.

It is doubtless one of Aristotle's great services that he conceived so clearly the truth that literature is a thing that grows and has a history. But no writer, certainly no ancient writer, is always vigilant. Sometimes Aristotle analyses his terms, but very often he takes them for granted; and in the latter case, I think, he is sometimes deceived by them. Thus there seem to be cases where he has been affected in his conceptions of fifth-century tragedy by the practice of his own day, when the only living form of drama was the New Comedy.

For example, as we have noticed above, true Tragedy had always taken its material from the sacred myths, or heroic sagas, which to the classical Greek constituted history. But the New Comedy was in the habit of inventing its plots. Consequently Aristotle falls into using the word mythos practically in the sense of 'plot', and writing otherwise in a way that is unsuited to the tragedy of the fifth century. He says that tragedy adheres to 'the historical names' for an aesthetic reason, because what has happened is obviously possible and therefore convincing. The real reason was that the drama and the myth were simply two different expressions of the same religious kernel. Again, he says of the Chorus that it should be an integral part of the play, which is true; but he also says that it' should be regarded as one of the actors', which shows to what an extent the Chorus in his day was dead and its technique forgotten.

He had lost the sense of what the Chorus was in the hands of the great masters, say in the Bacchae or the Eumenides. He mistakes, again, the use of that epiphany of a God which is frequent at the end of the single plays of Euripides, and which seems to have been equally so at the end of the trilogies of Aeschylus. Having lost the living tradition, he sees neither the ritual origin nor the dramatic value of these divine epiphanies. He thinks of the convenient gods and abstractions who sometimes spoke the prologues of the New Comedy, and imagines that the God appears in order to unravel the plot. As a matter of fact, in one play which he often quotes, the Iphigenia Taurica, the plot is actually distorted at the very end in order to give an opportunity for the epiphany. One can see the effect of the tradition also in his treatment of the terms Anagnorisis and Peripeteia, which Professor Bywater translates as 'Discovery and Peripety' and Professor Butcher as 'Recognition and Reversal of Fortune'. Aristotle assumes that these two elements are normally present in any tragedy, except those which he calls 'simple'; we may say, roughly, in any tragedy that really has a plot.

This strikes a modern reader as a very arbitrary assumption. Reversals of Fortune of some sort are perhaps usual in any varied plot, but surely not Recognitions? The clue to the puzzle lies, it can scarcely be doubted, in the historical origin of tragedy. Tragedy, according to Greek tradition, is originally the ritual play of Dionysus, performed at his festival, and representing, as Herodotus tells us, the 'sufferings' or 'passion' of that God. We are never directly told what these 'sufferings' were which were so represented; but Herodotus remarks that he found in Egypt a ritual that was 'in almost all points the same'. This was the well-known ritual of Osiris, in which the god was torn in pieces, lamented, searched for, discovered or recognized, and the mourning by a sudden Reversal turned into joy.

In any tragedy which still retained the stamp of its Dionysiac origin, this Discovery and Peripety might normally be expected to occur, and to occur together. I have tried to show elsewhere how many of our extant tragedies do, as a matter of fact, show the marks of this ritual. I hope it is not rash to surmise that the much-debated word katharsis, 'purification' or 'purgation', may have come into Aristotle's mouth from the same source.

It has all the appearance of being an old word which is accepted and re-interpreted by Aristotle rather than a word freely chosen by him to denote the exact phenomenon he wishes to describe. At any rate the Dionysus ritual itself was a katharmos or katharsis—a purification of the community from the taints and poisons of the past year, the old contagion of sin and death.

And the words of Aristotle's definition of tragedy in Chapter VI might have been used in the days of Thespis in a much cruder and less metaphorical sense. According to primitive ideas, the mimic representation on the stage of 'incidents arousing pity and fear' did act as a katharsis of such 'passions' or 'sufferings' in real life. (For the word pathemata means 'sufferings' as well as 'passions'.) It is worth remembering that in the year 361 B.C., during Aristotle's lifetime, Greek tragedies were introduced into Rome, not on artistic but on superstitious grounds, as a katharmos against a pestilence (Livy vii. 2). One cannot but suspect that in his account of the purpose of tragedy Aristotle may be using an old traditional formula, and consciously or unconsciously investing it with a new meaning, much as he has done with the word mythos.

Apart from these historical causes of misunderstanding, a good teacher who uses this book with a class will hardly fail to point out numerous points on which two equally good Greek scholars may well differ in the mere interpretation of the words. What, for instance, are the 'two natural causes' in Chapter IV which have given birth to Poetry? Are they, as our translator takes them, that man is imitative, and that people delight in imitations? Or are they that man is imitative and people delight in imitations, and the instinct for rhythm, as Professor Butcher prefers? Is it a 'creature' a thousand miles long, or a 'picture' a thousand miles long which raises some trouble in Chapter VII? The word zoon means equally 'picture' and 'animal'. Did the older poets make their characters speak like 'statesmen', politikoi, or merely like ordinary citizens, politai, while the moderns made theirs like 'professors of rhetoric'? It may seem as if the large uncertainties which we have indicated detract in a ruinous manner from the value of the Poetics to us as a work of criticism.

Certainly if any young writer took this book as a manual of rules by which to 'commence poet', he would find himself embarrassed. But, if the book is properly read, not as a dogmatic text-book but as a first attempt, made by a man of astounding genius, to build up in the region of creative art a rational order like that which he established in logic, rhetoric, ethics, politics, physics, psychology, and almost every department of knowledge that existed in his day, then the uncertainties become rather a help than a discouragement. They gave us occasion to think and use our imagination. They make us, to the best of our powers, try really to follow and criticize closely the bold gropings of an extraordinary thinker; and it is in this process, and not in any mere collection of dogmatic results, that we shall find the true value and beauty of the Poetics.

The book is of permanent value as a mere intellectual achievement; as a store of information about Greek literature; and as an original or first-hand statement of what we may call the classical view of artistic criticism. It does not regard poetry as a matter of unanalysed inspiration; it makes no concession to personal whims or fashion or ennui. It tries by rational methods to find out what is good in art and what makes it good, accepting the belief that there is just as truly a good way, and many bad ways, in poetry as in morals or in playing billiards. This is no place to try to sum up its main conclusions. But it is characteristic of the classical view that Aristotle lays his greatest stress, first, on the need for Unity in the work of art, the need that each part should subserve the whole, while irrelevancies, however brilliant in themselves, should be cast away; and next, on the demand that great art must have for its subject the great way of living.

These judgements have often been misunderstood, but the truth in them is profound and goes near to the heart of things. Characteristic, too, is the observation that different kinds of art grow and develop, but not indefinitely; they develop until they 'attain their natural form'; also the rule that each form of art should produce 'not every sort of pleasure but its proper pleasure'; and the sobre language in which Aristotle, instead of speaking about the sequence of events in a tragedy being 'inevitable', as we bombastic moderns do, merely recommends that they should be 'either necessary or probable' and 'appear to happen because of one another'. Conceptions and attitudes of mind such as these constitute what we may call the classical faith in matters of art and poetry; a faith which is never perhaps fully accepted in any age, yet, unlike others, is never forgotten but lives by being constantly criticized, re-asserted, and rebelled against. For the fashions of the ages vary in this direction and that, but they vary for the most part from a central road which was struck out by the imagination of Greece.

ARISTOTLE ON THE ART OF POETRY

Our subject being Poetry, I propose to speak not only of the art in general but also of its species and their respective capacities; of the structure of plot required for a good poem; of the number and nature of the constituent parts of a poem; and likewise of any other matters in the same line of inquiry. Let us follow the natural order and begin with the primary facts.

Epic poetry and Tragedy, as also Comedy, Dithyrambic poetry, and most flute-playing and lyre-playing, are all, viewed as a whole, modes of imitation. But at the same time they differ from one another in three ways, either by a difference of kind in their means, or by differences in the objects, or in the manner of their imitations.

- Just as form and colour are used as means by some, who (whether by art or constant practice) imitate and portray many things by their aid, and the voice is used by others; so also in the above-mentioned group of arts, the means with them as a whole are rhythm, language, and harmony—used, however, either singly or in certain combinations.

A combination of rhythm and harmony alone is the means in flute-playing and lyre-playing, and any other arts there may be of the same description, e.g. imitative piping. Rhythm alone, without harmony, is the means in the dancer's imitations; for even he, by the rhythms of his attitudes, may represent men's characters, as well as what they do and suffer. There is further an art which imitates by language alone, without harmony, in prose or in verse, and if in verse, either in some one or in a plurality of meters. This form of imitation is to this day without a name. We have no common name for a mime of Sophron or Xenarchus and a Socratic Conversation; and we should still be without one even if the imitation in the two instances were in trimeters or elegiacs or some other kind of verse—though it is the way with people to tack on 'poet' to the name of a meter, and talk of elegiac-poets and epic-poets, thinking that they call them poets not by reason of the imitative nature of their work, but indiscriminately by reason of the meter they write in.

Even if a theory of medicine or physical philosophy be put forth in a metrical form, it is usual to describe the writer in this way; Homer and Empedocles, however, have really nothing in common apart from their meter; so that, if the one is to be called a poet, the other should be termed a physicist rather than a poet. We should be in the same position also, if the imitation in these instances were in all the meters, like the Centaur (a rhapsody in a medley of all meters) of Chaeremon; and Chaeremon one has to recognize as a poet. So much, then, as to these arts. There are, lastly, certain other arts, which combine all the means enumerated, rhythm, melody, and verse, e.g.

Dithyrambic and Nomic poetry, Tragedy and Comedy; with this difference, however, that the three kinds of means are in some of them all employed together, and in others brought in separately, one after the other. These elements of difference in the above arts I term the means of their imitation.

- The objects the imitator represents are actions, with agents who are necessarily either good men or bad—the diversities of human character being nearly always derivative from this primary distinction, since the line between virtue and vice is one dividing the whole of mankind. It follows, therefore, that the agents represented must be either above our own level of goodness, or beneath it, or just such as we are in the same way as, with the painters, the personages of Polygnotus are better than we are, those of Pauson worse, and those of Dionysius just like ourselves. It is clear that each of the above-mentioned arts will admit of these differences, and that it will become a separate art by representing objects with this point of difference.

Even in dancing, flute-playing, and lyre-playing such diversities are possible; and they are also possible in the nameless art that uses language, prose or verse without harmony, as its means; Homer's personages, for instance, are better than we are; Cleophon's are on our own level; and those of Hegemon of Thasos, the first writer of parodies, and Nicochares, the author of the Diliad, are beneath it. The same is true of the Dithyramb and the Nome: the personages may be presented in them with the difference exemplified in the... of... and Argas, and in the Cyclopses of Timotheus and Philoxenus. This difference it is that distinguishes Tragedy and of the present day.

- A third difference in these arts is in the manner in which each kind of object is represented. Given both the same means and the same kind of object for imitation, one may either (1) speak at one moment in narrative and at another in an assumed character, as Homer does; or (2) one may remain the same throughout, without any such change; or (3) the imitators may represent the whole story dramatically, as though they were actually doing the things described.

As we said at the beginning, therefore, the differences in the imitation of these arts come under three heads, their means, their objects, and their manner. So that as an imitator Sophocles will be on one side akin to Homer, both portraying good men; and on another to Aristophanes, since both present their personages as acting and doing. This in fact, according to some, is the reason for plays being termed dramas, because in a play the personages act the story. Hence too both Tragedy and Comedy are claimed by the Dorians as their discoveries; Comedy by the Megarians—by those in Greece as having arisen when Megara became a democracy, and by the Sicilian Megarians on the ground that the poet Epicharmus was of their country, and a good deal earlier than Chionides and Magnes; even Tragedy also is claimed by certain of the Peloponnesian Dorians. In support of this claim they point to the words 'comedy' and 'drama'. Their word for the outlying hamlets, they say, is comae, whereas Athenians call them demes—thus assuming that comedians got the name not from their comoe or revels, but from their strolling from hamlet to hamlet, lack of appreciation keeping them out of the city. Their word also for 'to act', they say, is dran, whereas Athenians use prattein.

So much, then, as to the number and nature of the points of difference in the imitation of these arts. It is clear that the general origin of poetry was due to two causes, each of them part of human nature. Imitation is natural to man from childhood, one of his advantages over the lower animals being this, that he is the most imitative creature in the world, and learns at first by imitation. And it is also natural for all to delight in works of imitation.

The truth of this second point is shown by experience: though the objects themselves may be painful to see, we delight to view the most realistic representations of them in art, the forms for example of the lowest animals and of dead bodies. The explanation is to be found in a further fact: to be learning something is the greatest of pleasures not only to the philosopher but also to the rest of mankind, however small their capacity for it; the reason of the delight in seeing the picture is that one is at the same time learning--gathering the meaning of things, e.g. that the man there is so-and-so; for if one has not seen the thing before, one's pleasure will not be in the picture as an imitation of it, but will be due to the execution or colouring or some similar cause. Imitation, then, being natural to us—as also the sense of harmony and rhythm, the meters being obviously species of rhythms—it was through their original aptitude, and by a series of improvements for the most part gradual on their first efforts, that they created poetry out of their improvisations.

Poetry, however, soon broke up into two kinds according

to the differences of character in the individual poets; for the graver among them would represent noble actions, and those of noble personages; and the meaner sort the actions of the ignoble. The latter class produced invectives at first, just as others did hymns and panegyrics. We know of no such poem by any of the pre-Homeric poets, though there were probably many such writers among them; instances, however, may be found from Homer downwards, e.g. his Margites, and the similar poems of others. In this poetry of invective its natural fitness brought an iambic meter into use; hence our present term 'iambic', because it was the meter of their 'iambs' or invectives against one another.

The result was that the old poets became some of them writers of heroic and others of iambic verse. Homer's position, however, is peculiar: just as he was in the serious style the poet of poets, standing alone not only through the literary excellence, but also through the dramatic character of his imitations, so too he was the first to outline for us the general forms of Comedy by producing not a dramatic invective, but a dramatic picture of the Ridiculous; his Margites in fact stands in the same relation to our comedies as the Iliad and Odyssey to our tragedies. As soon, however, as Tragedy and Comedy appeared in the field, those naturally drawn to the one line of poetry became writers of comedies instead of iambs, and those naturally drawn to the other, writers of tragedies instead of epics, because these new modes of art were grander and of more esteem than the old. If it be asked whether Tragedy is now all that it need be in its formative elements, to consider that, and decide it theoretically and in relation to the theatres, is a matter for another inquiry.

It certainly began in improvisations—as did also Comedy; the one originating with the authors of the Dithyramb, the other with those of the phallic songs, which still survive as institutions in many of our cities. And its advance after that was little by little, through their improving on whatever they had before them at each stage. It was in fact only after a long series of changes that the movement of Tragedy stopped on its attaining to its natural form.

- The number of actors was first increased to two by Aeschylus, who curtailed the business of the Chorus, and made the dialogue, or spoken portion, take the leading part in the play.
- A third actor and scenery were due to Sophocles.
- Tragedy acquired also its magnitude. Discarding short stories and a ludicrous diction, through its passing out of its satyric stage, it assumed, though only at a late point in its progress, a tone of dignity; and its meter changed then from trochaic to iambic. The reason for their original use of the trochaic tetrameter was that their poetry was satyric and more connected with dancing than it now is. As soon, however, as a spoken part came in, nature herself found the appropriate meter. The iambic, we know, is the most speakable of meters, as is shown by the fact that we very often fall into it in conversation, whereas we rarely talk hexameters, and only when we depart from the speaking tone of voice.
- Another change was a plurality of episodes or acts. As for the remaining matters, the superadded embellishments and the account of their introduction, these must be taken as said, as it would probably be a long piece of work to go through the details.

As for Comedy, it is (as has been observed) an imitation of men worse than the average; worse, however, not as regards any and every sort of fault, but only as regards one particular kind, the Ridiculous, which is a species of the Ugly. The Ridiculous may be defined as a mistake or deformity not productive of pain or harm to others; the mask, for instance, that excites laughter, is something ugly and distorted without causing pain.

Though the successive changes in Tragedy and their authors are not unknown, we cannot say the same of Comedy; its early stages passed unnoticed, because it was not as yet taken up in a serious way. It was only at a late point in its progress that a chorus of comedians was officially granted by the archon; they used to be mere volunteers. It had also already certain definite forms at the time when the record of those termed comic poets begins. Who it was who supplied it with masks, or prologues, or a plurality of actors and the like, has remained unknown. The invented Fable, or Plot, however, originated in Sicily, with Epicharmus and Phormis; of Athenian poets Crates was the first to drop the Comedy of invective and frame stories of a general and non-personal nature, in other words, Fables or Plots.

Epic poetry, then, has been seen to agree with Tragedy to thi.e.tent, that of being an imitation of serious subjects in a grand kind of verse. It differs from it, however, in that it is in one kind of verse and in narrative form; and in its length—which is due to its action having no fixed limit of time, whereas Tragedy endeavours to keep as far as possible within a single circuit of the sun, or something near that. This, I say, is another point of difference between them, though at first the practice in this respect was just the same in tragedies as i.e.ic poems. They differ also in their constituents, some being common to both and others peculiar to Tragedy—hence a judge of good and bad in Tragedy is a judge of that i.e.ic poetry also. All the parts of an epic are included in Tragedy; but those of Tragedy are not all of them to be found in the Epic. Reserving hexameter poetry and Comedy for consideration hereafter, let us proceed now to the discussion of Tragedy; before doing so, however, we must gather up the definition resulting from what has been said.

A tragedy, then, is the imitation of an action that is serious and also, as having magnitude, complete in itself; in language with pleasurable accessories, each kind brought in separately in the parts of the work; in a dramatic, not in a narrative form; with incidents arousing pity and fear, wherewith to accomplish its catharsis of such emotions. Here by 'language with pleasurable accessories' I mean that with rhythm and harmony or song superadded; and by 'the kinds separately' I mean that some portions are worked out with verse only, and others in turn with song.

- As they act the stories, it follows that in the first place the Spectacle (or stage-appearance of the actors) must be some part of the whole; and in the second Melody and Diction, these two being the means of their imitation.

Here by 'Diction' I mean merely this, the composition of the verses; and by 'Melody', what is too completely understood to require explanation. But further: the subject represented also is an action; and the action involves agents, who must necessarily have their distinctive qualities both of character and thought, since it is from these that we ascribe certain qualities to their actions. There are in the natural order of things, therefore, two causes, Character and Thought, of their actions, and consequently of their success or failure in their lives. Now the action (that which was done) is represented in the play by the Fable or Plot.

The Fable, in our present sense of the term, is simply this, the combination of the incidents, or things done in the story; whereas Character is what makes us ascribe certain moral qualities to the agents; and Thought is shown in all they say when proving a particular point or, it may be, enunciating a general truth. There are six parts consequently of every tragedy, as a whole, that is, of such or such quality, viz. a Fable or Plot, Characters, Diction, Thought, Spectacle and Melody; two of them arising from the means, one from the manner, and three from the objects of the dramatic imitation; and there is nothing else besides these six. Of these, its formative elements, then, not a few of the dramatists have made due use, as every play, one may say, admits of Spectacle, Character, Fable, Diction, Melody, and Thought.

- The most important of the six is the combination of the incidents of the story.

Tragedy i.e.sentially an imitation not of persons but of action and life, of happiness and misery. All human happiness or misery takes the form of action; the end for which we live is a certain kind of activity, not a quality. Characte.g.ves us qualities, but it is in our actions—what we do—that we are happy or the reverse. In a play accordingly they do not act in order to portray the Characters; they include the Characters for the sake of the action. So that it is the action in it, i.e. its

Fable or Plot, that is the end and purpose of the tragedy; and the end i.e. everywhere the chief thing. Besides this, a tragedy is impossible without action, but there may be one without Character. The tragedies of most of the moderns are characterless—a defect common among poets of all kinds, and with its counterpart in painting in Zeuxis as compared with Polygnotus; for whereas the latter is strong in character, the work of Zeuxis is devoid of it. And again: one may string together a series of characteristic speeches of the utmost finish as regards Diction and Thought, and yet fail to produce the true tragi.e.fect; but one will have much better success with a tragedy which, however inferior in these respects, has a Plot, a combination of incidents, in it. And again: the most powerful elements of attraction in Tragedy, the Peripeties and Discoveries, are parts of the Plot. A further proof is in the fact that beginners succeed earlier with the Diction and Characters than with the construction of a story; and the same may be said of nearly all the early dramatists.

We maintain, therefore, that the first essential, the life and soul, so to speak, of Tragedy is the Plot; and that the Characters come second—compare the parallel in painting, where the most beautiful colours laid on without order will not give one the same pleasure as a simple black-and-white sketch of a portrait. We maintain that Tragedy is primarily an imitation of action, and that it is mainly for the sake of the action that it imitates the personal agents. Third comes the element of Thought, i.e. the power of saying whatever can be said, or what is appropriate to the occasion. This is what, in the speeches in Tragedy, falls under the arts of Politics and Rhetoric; for the older poets make their personages discourse like statesmen, and the moderns like rhetoricians. One must not confuse it with Character.

Character in a play is that which reveals the moral purpose of the agents, i.e. the sort of thing they seek or avoid, where that is not obvious—hence there is no room for Character in a speech on a purely indifferent subject. Thought, on the other hand, is shown in all they say when proving or disproving some particular point, or enunciating some universal proposition. Fourth among the literary elements is the Diction of the personages, i.e. as before explained, the expression of their thoughts in words, which is practically the same thing with verse as with prose. As for the two remaining parts, the Melody is the greatest of the pleasurable accessories of Tragedy. The Spectacle, though an attraction, is the least artistic of all the parts, and has least to do with the art of poetry.

The tragi.e.fect is quite possible without a public performance and actors; and besides, the getting-up of the Spectacle is more a matter for the costumier than the poet. Having thus distinguished the parts, let us now consider the proper construction of the Fable or Plot, as that is at once the first and the most important thing in Tragedy. We have laid it down that a tragedy is an imitation of an action that is complete in itself, as a whole of some magnitude; for a whole may be of no magnitude to speak of. Now a whole is that which has beginning, middle, and end. A beginning is that which is not itself necessarily after anything else, and which has naturally something else after it; an end is that which is naturally after something itself, either as its necessary or usual consequent, and with nothing else after it; and a middle, that which is by nature after one thing and has also another after it. A well-constructed Plot, therefore, cannot either begin or end at any point one likes; beginning and end in it must be of the forms just described. Again: to be beautiful, a living creature, and every whole made up of parts, must not only present a certain order in its arrangement of parts, but also be of a certain definite magnitude.

Beauty is a matter of size and order, and therefore impossible either in a very minute creature, since our perception becomes indistinct as it approaches instantaneity; or in a creature of vast size—one, say, 1,000 miles long—as in that case, instead of the object being seen all at once, the unity and wholeness of it is lost to the beholder. Just in the same way, then, as a beautiful whole made up of parts, or a beautiful living creature, must be of some size, a size to be taken in by the eye, so a story or Plot must be of some length, but of a length to be taken in by the memory. As for the limit of its length, so far as that is relative to public performances and spectators, it does not fall within the theory of poetry. If they had to perform a hundred tragedies, they would be timed by water-clocks, as they are said to have been at one period. The limit, however, set by the actual nature of the thing is this: the longer the story, consistently with its being comprehensible as a whole, the finer it is by reason of its magnitude. As a rough general formula, 'a length which allows of the hero passing by a series of probable or necessary stages from misfortune to happiness, or from happiness to misfortune', may suffice as a limit for the magnitude of the story.

The Unity of a Plot does not consist, as some suppose, in its having one man as its subject. An infinity of things befall that one man, some of which it is impossible to reduce to unity; and in like manner there are many actions of one man which cannot be made to form one action. One sees, therefore, the mistake of all the poets who have written a Heracleid, a Theseid, or similar poems; they suppose that, because Heracles was one man, the story also of Heracles must be one story. Homer, however, evidently understood this point quite well, whether by art or instinct, just in the same way as he excels the rest i.e.ery other respect. In writing an Odyssey, he did not make the poem cover all that ever befell his hero—it befell him, for instance, to get wounded on Parnassus and also to feign madness at the time of the call to arms, but the two incidents had no probable or necessary connexion with one another—instead of doing that, he took an action with a Unity of the kind we are describing as the subject of the Odyssey, as also of the Iliad.

The truth is that, just as in the other imitative arts one imitation is always of one thing, so in poetry the story, as an imitation of action, must represent one action, a complete whole, with its several incidents so closely connected that the transposal or withdrawal of any one of them will disjoin and dislocate the whole. For that which makes no perceptible difference by its presence or absence is no real part of the whole. From what we have said it will be seen that the poet's function is to describe, not the thing that has happened, but a kind of thing that might happen, i.e. what is possible as being probable or necessary. The distinction between historian and poet is not in the one writing prose and the other verse—you might put the work of Herodotus into verse, and it would still be a species of history; it consists really in this, that the one describes the thing that has been, and the other a kind of thing that might be. Hence poetry is something more philosophic and of graver import than history, since its statements are singulars.

By a universal statement I mean one as to what such or such a kind of man will probably or necessarily say or do—which is the aim of poetry, though it affixes proper names to the characters; by a singular statement, one as to what, say, Alcibiades did or had done to him. In Comedy this has become clear by this time; it is only when their plot is already made up of probable incidents that they give it a basis of proper names, choosing for the purpose any names that may occur to them, instead of writing like the old iambic poets about particular persons. In Tragedy, however, they still adhere to the historic names; and for this reason: what convinces is the possible; now whereas we are not yet sure as to the possibility of that which has not happened, that which has happened is manifestly possible, else it would not have come to pass. Nevertheless even in Tragedy there are some plays with but one or two known names in them, the rest being inventions; and there are some without a single known name, e.g.

Agathon's Anthens, in which both incidents and names are of the poet's invention; and it is no less delightful on that account. So that one must not aim at a rigid adherence to the traditional stories on which tragedies are based. It would be absurd, in fact, to do so, as even the known stories are only known to a few, though they are a delight none the less to all. It i.e.ident from the above that, the poet must be more the poet of his stories or Plots than of his verses, inasmuch as he is a poet by virtue of the imitative element in his work, and it is actions that he imitates. And if he should come to take a subject from actual history, he is none the less a poet for that; since some historic occurrences may very well be in the probable and possible order of things; and it is in that aspect of them that he is their poet. Of simple Plots and actions the episodic are the worst. I call a Plot episodic when there is neither probability nor necessity in the sequence of episodes.

Actions of this sort bad poets construct through their own fault, and good ones on account of the players. His work being for public performance, a good poet often stretches out a Plot beyond its capabilities, and is thus obliged to twist the sequence of incident. Tragedy, however, is an imitation not only of a complete action, but also of incidents arousing pity and fear. Such incidents have the very greatest effect on the mind when they occur unexpectedly and at the same time in consequence of one another; there is more of the marvellous in them then than if they happened of themselves or by mere chance. Even matters of chance seem most marvellous if there is an appearance of design as it were in them; as for instance the statue of Mitys at Argos killed the author of Mitys' death by falling down on him when a looker-on at a public spectacle; for incidents like that we think to be not without a meaning. A Plot, therefore, of this sort is necessarily finer than others.

Plots are either simple or complex, since the actions they represent are naturally of this twofold description. The action, proceeding in the way defined, as one continuous whole, I call simple, when the change in the hero's fortunes takes place without Peripety or Discovery; and complex, when it involves one or the other, or both. These should each of them arise out of the structure of the Plot itself, so as to be the consequence, necessary or probable, of the antecedents. There is a great difference between a thing happening propter hoc and post hoc. A Peripety is the change from one state of things within the play to its opposite of the kind described, and that too in the way we are saying, in the probable or necessary sequence of events; as it is for instance in Oedipus: here the opposite state of things is produced by the Messenger, who, coming to gladden Oedipus and to remove his fears as to his mother, reveals the secret of his birth. And in Lynceus: just as he is being led off for execution, with Danaus at his side to put him to death, the incidents preceding this bring it about that he is saved and Danaus put to death. A Discovery is, as the very word implies, a change from ignorance to knowledge, and thus to either love or hate, in the personages marked for good or evil fortune.

The finest form of Discovery is one attended by Peripeties, like that which goes with the Discovery in Oedipus. There are no doubt other forms of it; what we have said may happen in a way in reference to inanimate things, even things of a very casual kind; and it is also possible to discover whether some one has done or not done something. But the form most directly connected with the Plot and the action of the piece is the first-mentioned. This, with a Peripety, will arouse either pity or fear—actions of that nature being what Tragedy is assumed to represent; and it will also serve to bring about the happy or unhappy ending. The Discovery, then, being of persons, it may be that of one party only to the other, the latter being already known; or both the parties may have to discover themselves. Iphigenia, for instance, was discovered to Orestes by sending the letter; and another Discovery was required to reveal him to Iphigenia.

Two parts of the Plot, then, Peripety and Discovery, are on matters of this sort. A third part is Suffering; which we may define as an action of a destructive or painful nature, such as murders on the stage, tortures, woundings, and the like. The other two have been already explained. The parts of Tragedy to be treated as formative elements in the whole were mentioned in a previous Chapter. From the point of view, however, of its quantity, i.e. the separate sections into which it is divided, a tragedy has the following parts: Prologue, Episode, Exode, and a choral portion, distinguished into Parode and Stasimon; these two are common to all tragedies, whereas songs from the stage and Commoe are only found in some.

The Prologue is all that precedes the Parode of the chorus; an Episode all that comes in between two whole choral songs; the Exode all that follows after the last choral song. In the choral portion the Parode is the whole first statement of the chorus; a Stasimon, a song of the chorus without anapaests or trochees; a Commas, a lamentation sung by chorus and actor in concert. The parts of Tragedy to be used as formative elements in the whole we have already mentioned; the above are its parts from the point of view of its quantity, or the separate sections into which it is divided.

The next points after what we have said above will be these:

- What is the poet to aim at, and what is he to avoid, in constructing his Plots?
- What are the conditions on which the tragi.e.fect depends? We assume that, for the finest form of Tragedy, the Plot must be not simple but complex; and further, that it must imitate actions arousing pity and fear, since that is the distinctive function of this kind of imitation. It follows, therefore, that there are three forms of Plot to be avoided.
  - A good man must not be seen passing from happiness to misery,
  - A bad man from misery to happiness.

The first situation is not fear-inspiring or piteous, but simply odious to us. The second is the most untragic that can be; it has no one of the requisites of Tragedy; it does not appeal either to the human feeling in us, or to our pity, or to our fears. Nor, on the other hand, should (3) an extremely bad man be seen falling from happiness into misery. Such a story may arouse the human feeling in us, but it will not move us to either pity or fear; pity is occasioned by undeserved misfortune, and fear by that of one like ourselves; so that there will be nothing either piteous or fear-inspiring in the situation.

There remains, then, the intermediate kind of personage, a man not ɔre-eminently virtuous and just, whose misfortune, however, is brought upon him not by vice and depravity but by some error of judgement, of the number of those in the enjoyment of great reputation and prosperity; e.g. Oedipus, Thyestes, and the men of note of similar families. The perfect Plot, accordingly, must have a single, and not (as some tell us) a double issue; the change in the hero's fortunes must be not from misery to happiness, but on the contrary from happiness to misery; and the cause of it must lie not in any depravity, but in some great error on his part; the man himself being either such as we have described, or better, not worse, than that.

Fact also confirms our theory. Though the poets began by accepting any tragic story that came to hand, in these days the finest tragedies are always on the story of some few houses, on that of Alemeon, Oedipus, Orestes, Meleager, Thyestes, Telephus, or any others that may have been involved, as either agents or sufferers, in some deed of horror. The theoretically best tragedy, then, has a Plot of this description. The critics, therefore, are wrong who blame Euripides for taking this line in his tragedies, and giving many of them an unhappy ending. It is, as we have said, the right line to take. The best proof is this: on the stage, and in the public performances, such plays, properly worked out, are seen to be the most truly tragic; and Euripides, even if hi.e.ecution be faulty i.e.ery other point, is seen to be nevertheless the most tragic certainly of the dramatists. After this comes the construction of Plot which some rank first, one with a double story (like the Odyssey) and an opposite issue for the good and the bad personages.

It is ranked as first only through the weakness of the audiences; the poets merely follow their public, writing as its wishes dictate. But the pleasure here is not that of Tragedy. It belongs rather to Comedy, where the bitterest enemies in the piece (e.g. Orestes and Aegisthus) walk off good friends at the end, with no slaying of any one by any one. The tragic fear and pity may be aroused by the Spectacle; but they may also be aroused by the very structure and incidents of the play—which is the better way and shows the better poet. The Plot in fact should be so framed that, even without seeing the things take place, he who simply hears the account of them shall be filled with horror and pity at the incidents; which is just the effect that the mere recital of the story in Oedipus would have on one. To produce this same effect by means of the Spectacle is less artistic, and requires extraneous aid.

Those, however, who make use of the Spectacle to put before us that which is merely monstrous and not productive of fear, are wholly out of touch with Tragedy; not every kind of pleasure should be required of a tragedy, but only its own proper pleasure. The tragic pleasure is that of pity and fear, and the poet has to produce it by a work of imitation; it is clear, therefore, that the causes should be included in the incidents of his story. Let us see, then, what kinds of incident strike one as horrible, or rather as piteous. In a deed of this description the parties must necessarily be either friends, or enemies, or indifferent to one another.

Now when enemy does it on enemy, there is nothing to move us to pity either in his doing or in his meditating the deed, except so far as the actual pain of the sufferer is concerned; and the same is true when the parties are indifferent to one another. Whenever the tragic deed, however, is done within the family—when murder or the like is done or meditated by brother on brother, by son on father, by mother on son, or son on mother—these are the situations the poet should seek after.

The traditional stories, accordingly, must be kept as they are, e.g. the murder of Clytaemnestra by Orestes and of Eriphyle by Alcmeon. At the same time even with these there is something left to the poet himself; it is for him to devise the right way of treating them. Let us explain more clearly what we mean by 'the right way'. The deed of horror may be done by the doer knowingly and consciously, as in the old poets, and in Medea's murder of her children in Euripides. Or he may do it, but in ignorance of his relationship, and discover that afterwards, as does the Oedipus in Sophocles. Here the deed is outside the play; but it may be within it, like the act of the Alcmeon in Astydamas, or that of the Telegonus in Ulysses Wounded. A third possibility is for one meditating some deadly injury to another, in ignorance of his relationship, to make the discovery in time to draw back.

These exhaust the possibilities, since the deed must necessarily be either done or not done, and either knowingly or unknowingly. The worst situation is when the personage is with full knowledge on the point of doing the deed, and leaves it undone. It is odious and also (through the absence of suffering) untragic; hence it is that no one is made to act thus except in some few instances, e.g. Haemon and Creon in Antigone. Next after this comes the actual perpetration of the deed meditated. A better situation than that, however, is for the deed to be done in ignorance, and the relationship discovered afterwards, since there is nothing odious in it, and the Discovery will serve to astound us. But the best of all is the last; what we have in Cresphontes, for example, where Merope, on the point of slaying her son, recognizes him in time; in Iphigenia, where sister and brother are in a like position; and in Helle, where the son recognizes his mother, when on the point of giving her up to her enemy.

This will explain why our tragedies are restricted (as we said just now) to such a small number of families. It was accident rather than art that led the poets in quest of subjects to embody this kind of incident in their Plots. They are still obliged, accordingly, to have recourse to the families in which such horrors have occurred. On the construction of the Plot, and the kind of Plot required for Tragedy, enough has now been said. In the Characters there are four points to aim at. First and foremost, that they shall be good.

There will be an element of character in the play, if (as has been observed) what a personage says or does reveals a certain moral purpose; and a good element of character, if the purpose so revealed is good. Such goodness is possible i.e.ery type of personage, even in a woman or a slave, though the one is perhaps an inferior, and the other a wholly worthless being. The second point is to make them appropriate. The Character before us may be, say, manly; but it is not appropriate in a female Character to be manly, or clever. The third is to make them like the reality, which is not the same as their being good and appropriate, in our sense of the term. The fourth is to make them consistent and the same throughout; even if inconsistency be part of the man before one for imitation as presenting that form of character, he should still be consistently inconsistent.

We have an instance of baseness of character, not required for the story, in the Menelaus in Orestes; of the incongruous and unbefitting in the lamentation of Ulysses in Scylla, and in the (clever) speech of Melanippe; and of inconsistency in Iphigenia at Aulis, where Iphigenia the suppliant is utterly unlike the later Iphigenia. The right thing, however, is in the Characters just as in the incidents of the play to endeavour always after the necessary or the probable; so that whenever such-and-such a personage says or does such-and-such a thing, it shall be the probable or necessary outcome of his character; and whenever this incident follows on that, it shall be either the necessary or the probable consequence of it.

From this one sees (to digress for a moment) that the Denouement also should arise out of the plot itself, arid not depend on a stage-artifice, as in Medea, or in the story of the (arrested) departure of the Greeks in the Iliad. The artifice must be reserved for matters outside the play—for past events beyond human knowledge, or events yet to come, which require to be foretold or announced; since it is the privilege of the Gods to know everything. There should be nothing improbable among the actual incidents.

If it be unavoidable, however, it should be outside the tragedy, like the improbability in the Oedipus of Sophocles. But to return to the Characters. As Tragedy is an imitation of personages better than the ordinary man, we in our way should follow the example of good portrait-painters, who reproduce the distinctive features of a man, and at the same time, without losing the likeness, make him handsomer than he is. The poet in like manner, in portraying men quick or slow to anger, or with similar infirmities of character, must know how to represent them as such, and at the same time as good men, as Agathon and Homer have represented Achilles. All these rules one must keep in mind throughout, and further, those also for such points of stage-effect as directly depend on the art of the poet, since in these too one may often make mistakes. Enough, however, has been said on the subject in one of our published writings.

Discovery in general has been explained already. As for the species of Discovery, the first to be noted is the least artistic form of it, of which the poets make most use through mere lack of invention, Discovery by signs or marks. Of these signs some are congenital, like the 'lance-head which the Earth-born have on them', or 'stars', such as Carcinus brings in in his Thyestes; others acquired after birth— these latter being either marks on the body, e.g. scars, or external tokens, like necklaces, or to take another sort of instance, the ark in the Discovery in Tyro. Even these, however, admit of two uses, a better and a worse; the scar of Ulysses is an instance; the Discovery of him through it is made in one way by the nurse and in another by the swineherds.

A Discovery using signs as a means of assurance is less artistic, as indeed are all such as imply reflection; whereas one bringing them in all of a sudden, as in the Bath-story, is of a better order. Next after these are Discoveries made directly by the poet; which are inartistic for that very reason; e.g. Orestes' Discovery of himself in Iphigenia: whereas his sister reveals who she is by the letter, Orestes is made to say himself what the poet rather than the story demands.

This, therefore, is not far removed from the first-mentioned fault, since he might have presented certain tokens as well. Another instance is the 'shuttle's voice' in the Tereus of Sophocles. A third species is Discovery through memory, from a man's consciousness being awakened by something seen or heard. Thus in The Cyprioe of Dicaeogenes, the sight of the picture makes the man burst into tears; and in the Tale of Alcinous, hearing the harper Ulysses is reminded of the past and weeps; the Discovery of them being the result. A fourth kind is Discovery through reasoning; e.g. in The Choephoroe: 'One like me is here; there is no one like me but Orestes; he, therefore, must be here.' Or that which Polyidus the Sophist suggested for Iphigenia; since it was natural for Orestes to reflect: 'My sister was sacrificed, and I am to be sacrificed like her.' Or that in the Tydeus of Theodectes: 'I came to find a son, and am to die myself.'

Or that in The Phinidae: on seeing the place the women inferred their fate, that they were to die there, since they had also been exposed there. There is, too, a composite Discovery arising from bad reasoning on the side of the other party. An instance of it is in Ulysses the False Messenger: he said he should know the bow—which he had not seen; but to suppose from that that he would know it again (as though he had once seen it) was bad reasoning. The best of all Discoveries, however, is that arising from the incidents themselves, when the great surprise comes about through a probable incident, like that in the Oedipus of Sophocles; and also in Iphigenia; for it was not improbable that she should wish to have a letter taken home. These last are the only Discoveries independent of the artifice of signs and necklaces. Next after them come Discoveries through reasoning.

At the time when he is constructing his Plots, and engaged on the Diction in which they are worked out, the poet should remember to put the actual scenes as far as possible before he sees. In this way, seeing everything with the vividness of an eye-witness as it were, he will devise what is appropriate, and be least likely to overlook incongruities. This is shown by what was censured in Carcinus, the return of Amphiaraus from the sanctuary; it would have passed unnoticed, if it had not been actually seen by the audience; but on the stage his play failed, the incongruity of the incident offending the spectators. As far as may be, too, the poet should even act his story with the very gestures of his personages.

Given the same natural qualifications, he who feels the emotions to be described will be the most convincing; distress and anger, for instance, are portrayed most truthfully by one who is feeling them at the moment. Hence it is that poetry demands a man with special gift for it, or else one with a touch of madness in him; the, former can easily assume the required mood, and the latter may be actually beside himself with emotion. His story, again, whether already made or of his own making, he should first simplify and reduce to a universal form, before proceeding to lengthen it out by the insertion of episodes.

The following will show how the universal element in Iphigenia, for instance, may be viewed: A certain maiden having been offered in sacrifice, and spirited away from her sacrificers into another land, where the custom was to sacrifice all strangers to the Goddess, she was made there the priestess of this rite. Long after that the brother of the priestess happened to come; the fact, however, of the oracle having for a certain reason bidden him go thither, and his object in going, are outside the Plot of the play. On his coming he was arrested, and about to be sacrificed, when he revealed who he was—either as Euripides puts it, or (as suggested by Polyidus) by the not improbable exclamation, 'So I too am doomed to be sacrificed, as my sister was'; and the disclosure led to his salvation. This done, the next thing, after the proper names have been fixed as a basis for the story, is to work in episodes or accessory incidents. One must mind, however, that the episodes are appropriate, like the fit of madness in Orestes, which led to his arrest, and the purifying, which brought about his salvation. In plays, then, the episodes are short; i.e.ic poetry they serve to lengthen out the poem. The argument of the Odyssey is not a long one. A certain man has been abroad many years; Poseidon i.e.er on the watch for him, and he is all alone. Matters at home too have come to this, that his substance is being wasted and his son's death plotted by suitors to his wife. Then he arrives there himself after his grievous sufferings; reveals himself, and falls on his enemies; and the end is his salvation and their death.

This being all that is proper to the Odyssey, everything else in it is episode. There is a further point to be borne in mind. Every tragedy is in part Complication and in part Denouement; the incidents before the opening scene, and often certain also of those within the play, forming the Complication; and the rest the Denouement. By Complication I mean all from the beginning of the story to the point just before the change in the hero's fortunes; by Denouement, all from the beginning of the change to the end. In the Lynceus of Theodectes, for instance, the Complication includes, together with the presupposed incidents, the seizure of the child and that in turn of the parents; and the Denouement all from the indictment for the murder to the end.

Now it is right, when one speaks of a tragedy as the same or not the same as another, to do so on the ground before all else of their Plot, i.e. as having the same or not the same

Complication and Denouement. Yet there are many dramatists who, after a good Complication, fail in the Denouement. But it is necessary for both points of construction to be always duly mastered. There are four distinct species of Tragedy—that being the number of the constituents also that have been mentioned: first, the complex Tragedy, which is all Peripety and Discovery; second, the Tragedy of suffering, e.g. the Ajaxes and Ixions; third, the Tragedy of character, e.g. The Phthiotides and Peleus. The fourth constituent is that of 'Spectacle', exemplified in The Phorcides, in Prometheus, and in all plays with the scene laid in the nether world.

The poet's aim, then, should be to combine every element of interest, if possible, or else the more important and the major part of them. This is now especially necessary owing to the unfair criticism to which the poet is subjected in these days. Just because there have been poets before him strong in the several species of tragedy, the critics now expect the one man to surpass that which was the strong point of each one of his predecessors. One should also remember what has been said more than once, and not write a tragedy on an epic body of incident (i.e. one with a plurality of stories in it), by attempting to dramatize, for instance, the entire story of the Iliad.

In the epic owing to its scale every part is treated at proper length; with a drama, however, on the same story the result is very disappointing. This is shown by the fact that all who have dramatized the fall of Ilium in its entirety, and not part by part, like Euripides, or the whole of the Niobe story, instead of a portion, like Aeschylus, either fail utterly or have but ill success on the stage; for that and that alone was enough to rui.e.en a play by Agathon. Yet in their Peripeties, as also in their simple plots, the poets I mean show wonderful skill in aiming at the kind of effect they desire—a tragic situation that arouses the human feeling in one, like the clever villain (e.g. Sisyphus) deceived, or the brave wrongdoer worsted. This is probable, however, only in Agathon's sense, when he speaks of the probability of even improbabilities coming to pass.

The Chorus too should be regarded as one of the actors; it should be an integral part of the whole, and take a share in the action—that which it has in Sophocles rather than in Euripides. With the later poets, however, the songs in a play of theirs have no more to do with the Plot of that than of any other tragedy. Hence it is that they are now singing intercalary pieces, a practice first introduced by Agathon. And yet what real difference is there between singing such intercalary pieces, and attempting to fit in a speech, or even a whole act, from one play into another? The Plot and Characters having been discussed, it remains to consider the Diction and Thought. As for the Thought, we may assume what is said of it in our Art of Rhetoric, as it belongs more properly to that department of inquiry.

The Thought of the personages is shown in everything to be effected by their language—in every effort to prove or disprove, to arouse emotion (pity, fear, anger, and the like), or to maximize or minimize things. It is clear, also, that their mental procedure must be on the same lines in their actions likewise, whenever they wish them to arouse pity or horror, or have a look of importance or probability. The only difference is that with the act the impression has to be made without explanation; whereas with the spoken word it has to be produced by the speaker, and result from his language.

What, indeed, would be the good of the speaker, if things appeared in the required light even apart from anything he says? As regards the Diction, one subject for inquiry under this head is the turns given to the language when spoken; e.g. the difference between command and prayer, simple statement and threat, question and answer, and so forth. The theory of such matters, however, belongs to Elocution and the professors of that art. Whether the poet knows these things or not, his art as a poet is never seriously criticized on that account. What fault can one see in Homer's 'Sing of the wrath, Goddess'?—which Protagoras has criticized as being a command where a prayer was meant, since to bid one do or not do, he tells us, is a command. Let us pass over this, then, as appertaining to another art, and not to that of poetry.

The Diction viewed as a whole is made up of the following parts: the Letter (or ultimate element), the Syllable, the

Conjunction, the Article, the Noun, the Verb, the Case, and the Speech.

- The Letter is an indivisible sound of a particular kind, one that may become a factor in an intelligible sound. Indivisible sounds are uttered by the brutes also, but no one of these is a Letter in our sense of the term. These elementary sounds are either vowels, semivowels, or mutes. A vowel is a Letter having an audible sound without the addition of another Letter. A semivowel, one having an audible sound by the addition of another Letter; e.g. S and R. A mute, one having no sound at all by itself, but becoming audible by an addition, that of one of the Letters which have a sound of some sort of their own; e.g. D and G. The Letters differ in various ways: as produced by different conformations or in different regions of the mouth; as aspirated, not aspirated, or sometimes one and sometimes the other; as long, short, or of variable quantity; and further as having an acute.g.ave, or intermediate accent. The details of these matters we must leave to the metricians.
- A Syllable is a non significant composite sound, made up of a mute and a Letter having a sound (a vowel or semivowel); for GR, without an A, is just as much a Syllable as GRA, with an A. The various forms of the Syllable also belong to the theory of meter.
- A Conjunction is (a) a non-significant sound which, when one significant sound is formable out of several, neither hinders nor aids the union, and which, if the Speech thus formed stands by itself (apart from other Speeches) must not be inserted at the beginning of it; e.g. men, de, toi, de. Or (b) a non-significant sound capable of combining two or more significant sounds into one; e.g. amphi, peri, etc.
- An Article is a non-significant sound marking the beginning, end, or dividing-point of a Speech, its natural place being either at the extremities or in the middle.

- A Noun or name is a composite significant sound not involving the idea of time, with parts which have no significance by themselves in it. It is to be remembered that in a compound we do not think of the parts as having a significance also by themselves; in the name 'Theodorus', for instance, the doron means nothing to us.

A Verb is a composite significant sound involving the idea of time, with parts which (just as in the Noun) have no significance by themselves in it. Whereas the word 'man' or 'white' does not imply when, 'walks' and 'has walked' involve in addition to the idea of walking that of time present or time past. A Case of a Noun or Verb is when the word means 'of or 'to' a thing, and so forth, or for one or many (e.g. 'man' and 'men'); or it may consist merely in the mode of utterance, e.g. in question, command, etc. 'Walked?' and 'Walk!' are Cases of the verb 'to walk' of this last kind.

- A Speech is a composite significant sound, some of the parts of which have a certain significance by themselves. It may be observed that a Speech is not always made up of Noun and Verb; it may be without a Verb, like the definition of man; but it will always have some part with a certain significance by itself. In the Speech 'Cleon walks', 'Cleon' is an instance of such a part. A Speech is said to be one in two ways, either as signifying one thing, or as a union of several Speeches made into one by conjunction. Thus the Iliad is one Speech by conjunction of several; and the definition of man is one through its signifying one thing.

Nouns are of two kinds, either (1) simple, i.e. made up of non-significant parts, like the word ge, or (2) double; in the latter case the word may be made up either of a significant and a non-significant part (a distinction which disappears in the compound), or of two significant parts.

It is possible also to have triple, quadruple or higher compounds, like most of our amplified names; e.g.' Hermocaicoxanthus' and the like. Whatever its structure, a

Noun must always be either the ordinary word for the thing, or a strange word, or a metaphor, or an ornamental word, or a coined word, or a word lengthened out, or curtailed, or altered in form. By the ordinary word I mean that in general use in a country; and by a strange word, one in use elsewhere. So that the same word may obviously be at once strange and ordinary, though not in reference to the same people; sigunos, for instance, is an ordinary word in Cyprus, and a strange word with us. Metaphor consists in giving the thing a name that belongs to something else; the transference being either from genus to species, or from species to genus, or from species to species, or on grounds of analogy. That from genus to species i.e. emplified in 'Here stands my ship'; for lying at anchor is the 'standing' of a particular kind of thing.

That from species to genus in 'Truly ten thousand good deeds has Ulysses wrought', where 'ten thousand', which is a particular large number, is put in place of the generic 'a large number'. That from species to species in 'Drawing the life with the bronze', and in 'Severing with the enduring bronze'; where the poet uses 'draw' in the sense of 'sever' and 'sever' in that of 'draw', both words meaning to 'take away' something. That from analogy is possible whenever there are four terms so related that the second (B) is to the first (A), as the fourth (D) to the third (C); for one may then metaphorically put B in lieu of D, and D in lieu of B. Now and then, too, they qualify the metaphor by adding on to it that to which the word it supplants is relative.

Thus a cup (B) is in relation to Dionysus (A) what a shield (D) is to Ares (C). The cup accordingly will be metaphorically described as the 'shield of Dionysus' (D + A), and the shield as the 'cup of Ares' (B + C). Or to take another instance: As old age (D) is to life (C), so i.e.ening (B) to day (A). One will accordingly describe evening (B) as the 'old age of the day' (D + A)—or by the Empedoclean equivalent; and old age (D) as the 'evening' or 'sunset of life'' (B + C). It may be that some of the terms thus related have no special name of their own, but for all that they will be metaphorically described in just the same way. Thus to cast forth seed-corn is called 'sowing'; but to cast forth its flame, as said of the sun, has no special name. This nameless act (B), however, stands in just the same relation to its object, sunlight (A), as sowing (D) to the seed-corn (C). Hence the expression in the poet, 'sowing around a god-created flame' (D + A). There is also another form of qualified metaphor. Having given the thing the alien name, one may by a negative addition deny of it one of the attributes naturally associated with its new name. An instance of this would be to call the shield not the 'cup of Ares,' as in the former case, but a 'cup that holds no wine'. A coined word is a name which, being quite unknown among a people, is given by the poet himself; e.g. (for there are some words that seem to be of this origin) hernyges for horns, and areter for priest. A word is said to be lengthened out, when it has a short vowel made long, or an extra syllable inserted; e. g. polleos for poleos, Peleiadeo for Peleidon.

It is said to be curtailed, when it has lost a part; e.g. kri, do, and ops in mia ginetai amphoteron ops. It is an altered word, when part is left as it was and part is of the poet's making; e.g. dexiteron for dexion, in dexiteron kata maxon. The Nouns themselves (to whatever class they may belong) are either masculines, feminines, or intermediates (neuter). All ending in N, P, S, or in the two compounds of this last, PS and X, are masculines. All ending in the invariably long vowels, H and O, and in A among the vowels that may be long, are feminines. So that there is an equal number of masculine and feminine terminations, as PS and X are the same as S, and need not be counted. There is no Noun, however, ending in a mute or i.e.ther of the two short vowels, E and O. Only three (meli, kommi, peperi) end in I, and five in T. The intermediates, or neuters, end in the variable vowels or in N, P, X. The perfection of Diction is for it to be at once clear and not mean. The clearest indeed is that made up of the ordinary words for things, but it is mean, as is shown by the poetry of Cleophon and Sthenelus.

On the other hand the Diction becomes distinguished and non-prosaic by the use of unfamiliar terms, i.e. strange words, metaphors, lengthened forms, and everything that deviates from the ordinary modes of speech. But a whole statement in such terms will be either a riddle or a barbarism, a riddle, if made up of metaphors, a barbarism, if made up of strange words. The very nature indeed of a riddle is this, to describe a fact in an impossible combination of words (which cannot be done with the real names for things, but can be with their metaphorical substitutes); e.g. 'I saw a man glue brass on another with fire', and the like. The corresponding use of strange words results in a barbarism.—A certain admixture, accordingly, of unfamiliar terms is necessary.

These, the strange word, the metaphor, the ornamental equivalent, etc.. will save the language from seeming mean and prosaic, while the ordinary words in it will secure the requisite clearness. What helps most, however, to render the Diction at once clear and non-prosaic is the use of the lengthened, curtailed, and altered forms of words. Their deviation from the ordinary words will, by making the language unlike that in general use.g.ve it a non-prosaic appearance; and their having much in common with the words in general use will give it the quality of clearness. It is not right, then, to condemn these modes of speech, and ridicule the poet for using them, as some have done; e.g.

The elder Euclid, who said it was easy to make poetry if one were to be allowed to lengthen the words in the statement itself as much as one likes—a procedure he caricatured by reading 'Epixarhon eidon Marathonade Badi—gonta, and ouk han g' eramenos ton ekeinou helle boron as verses. A too apparent use of these licences has certainly a ludicrous effect, but they are not alone in that; the rule of moderation applies to all the constituents of the poetic vocabulary; even with metaphors, strange words, and the rest, the effect will be the same, if one uses them improperly and with a view to provoking laughter. The proper use of them is a very different thing.

To realise the difference one should take an epic verse and see how it reads when the normal words are introduced. The same should be done too with the strange word, the metaphor, and the rest; for one has only to put the ordinary words in their place to see the truth of what we are saying. The same iambic, for instance, is found in Aeschylus and Euripides, and as it stands in the former it is a poor line; whereas Euripides, by the change of a single word, the substitution of a strange for what is by usage the ordinary word, has made it seem a fine one. Aeschylus having said in his Philoctetes: phagedaina he mon sarkas hesthiei podos Euripides has merely altered the hesthiei here into thoinatai. Or suppose nun de m' heon holigos te kai outidanos kai haeikos to be altered by the substitution of the ordinary words into nun de m' heon mikros te kai hasthenikos kai haeidos Or the line diphron haeikelion katatheis olingen te trapexan into diphron moxtheron katatheis mikran te trapexan Or heiones boosin into heiones kraxousin.

Add to this that Ariphrades used to ridicule the tragedians for introducing expressions unknown in the language of common life, doeaton hapo (for apo domaton), sethen, hego de nin, Achilleos peri (for peri Achilleos), and the like. The mere fact of their not being in ordinary speech gives the Diction a non-prosaic character; but Ariphrades was unaware of that. It is a great thing, indeed, to make a proper use of these poetical forms, as also of compounds and strange words. But the greatest thing by far is to be a master of metaphor. It is the one thing that cannot be learnt from others; and it is also a sign of genius, since a good metaphor implies an intuitive perception of the similarity in dissimilars. Of the kinds of words we have enumerated it may be observed that compounds are most in place in the dithyramb, strange words in heroic, and metaphors in iambic poetry.

Heroic poetry, indeed, may avail itself of them all. But in iambic verse, which models itself as far as possible on the spoken language, only those kinds of words are in place which are allowable also in an oration, i.e. the ordinary word, the metaphor, and the ornamental equivalent. Let this, then, suffice as an account of Tragedy, the art imitating by means of action on the stage. As for the poetry which merely narrates, or imitates by means of versified language (without action), it is evident that it has several points in common with Tragedy.

- The construction of its stories should clearly be like

that in a drama; they should be based on a single action, one that is a complete whole in itself, with a beginning, middle, and end, so as to enable the work to produce its own proper pleasure with all the organic unity of a living creature. Nor should one suppose that there is anything like them in our usual histories. A history has to deal not with one action, but with one period and all that happened in that to one or more persons, however disconnected the several events may have been.

Just as two events may take place at the same time, e.g. the sea-fight off Salamis and the battle with the Carthaginians in Sicily, without converging to the same end, so too of two consecutive events one may sometimes come after the other with no one end as their common issue. Nevertheless most of our epic poets, one may say, ignore the distinction. Herein, then, to repeat what we have said before, we have a further proof of Homer's marvellous superiority to the rest. He did not attempt to deal even with the Trojan war in its entirety, though it was a whole with a definite beginning and end—through a feeling apparently that it was too long a story to be taken in in one view, or if not that, too complicated from the variety of incident in it.

As it is, he has singled out one section of the whole; many of the other incidents, however, he brings in as episodes, using the Catalogue of the Ships, for instance, and other episodes to relieve the uniformity of his narrative. As for the other epic poets, they treat of one man, or one period; or else of an action which, although one, has a multiplicity of parts in it. This last is what the authors of the Cypria and Little Iliad have done. And the result is that, whereas the Iliad or Odyssey supplies materials for only one, or at most two tragedies, the Cypria does that for several, and the Little Iliad for more than eight: for an Adjudgment of Arms, a Philoctetes, a Neoptolemus, a Eurypylus, a Ulysses as Beggar, a Laconian Women, a Fall of Ilium, and a Departure of the Fleet; as also a Sinon, and Women of Troy.

Besides this, Epic poetry must divide into the same species

as Tragedy; it must be either simple or complex, a story of character or one of suffering. Its parts, too, with the exception of Song and Spectacle, must be the same, as it requires Peripeties, Discoveries, and scenes of suffering just like Tragedy. Lastly, the Thought and Diction in it must be good in their way. All these elements appear in Homer first; and he has made due use of them. His two poems are each examples of construction, the Iliad simple and a story of suffering, the Odyssey complex (there is Discovery throughout it) and a story of character. And they are more than this, since in Diction and Thought too they surpass all other poems.

There is, however, a difference in the Epic as compared with Tragedy, in its length, and in its meter. As to its length, the limit already suggested will suffice: it must be possible for the beginning and end of the work to be taken in in one view—a condition which will be fulfilled if the poem be shorter than the old epics, and about as long as the series of tragedies offered for one hearing. For the extension of its length epic poetry has a special advantage, of which it makes large use.

In a play one cannot represent an action with a number of parts going on simultaneously; one is limited to the part on the stage and connected with the actors. Whereas i.e.ic poetry the narrative form makes it possible for one to describe a number of simultaneous incidents; and these, if germane to the subject, increase the body of the poem. This then is a gain to the Epic, tending to give it grandeur, and also variety of interest and room for episodes of diverse kinds. Uniformity of incident by the satiety it soon creates is apt to ruin tragedies on the stage. As for its meter, the heroic has been assigned it from experience; were any one to attempt a narrative poem in some one, or in several, of the other meters, the incongruity of the thing would be apparent.

The heroic; in fact is the gravest and weightiest of meters—which is what makes it more tolerant than the rest of strange words and metaphors, that also being a point in which the narrative form of poetry goes beyond all others. The iambic and trochaic, on the other hand, are meters of movement, the one representing that of life and action, the other that of the dance. Still more unnatural would it appear, it one were to write an epic in a medley of meters, as Chaeremon did. Hence it is that no one has ever written a long story in any but heroic verse; nature herself, as we have said, teaches us to select the meter appropriate to such a story.

Homer, admirable as he is in every other respect, is especially so in this, that he alone among epic poets is not unaware of the part to be played by the poet himself in the poem. The poet should say very little in propria persona, as he is no imitator when doing that. Whereas the other poets are perpetually coming forward in person, and say but little, and that only here and there, as imitators, Homer after a brief preface brings in forthwith a man, a woman, or some other Character—no one of them characterless, but each with distinctive characteristics. The marvellous is certainly required in Tragedy. The Epic, however, affords more opening for the improbable, the chief factor in the marvellous, because in it the agents are not visibly before one.

The scene of the pursuit of Hector would be ridiculous on the stage—the Greeks halting instead of pursuing him, and Achilles shaking his head to stop them; but in the poem the absurdity is overlooked. The marvellous, however, is a cause of pleasure, as is shown by the fact that we all tell a story with additions, in the belief that we are doing our hearers a pleasure. Homer more than any other has taught the rest of us the art of framing lies in the right way. I mean the use of paralogism. Whenever, if A is or happens, a consequent, B, is or happens, men's notion is that, if the B is, the A also is—but that is a false conclusion. Accordingly, if A is untrue, but there is something else, B, that on the assumption of its truth follows as its consequent, the right thing then is to add on the B. Just because we know the truth of the consequent, we are in our own minds led on to the erroneous inference of the truth of the antecedent. Here is an instance, from the Bath-story in the Odyssey.

A likely impossibility is always preferable to an unconvincing possibility. The story should never be made up of improbable incidents; there should be nothing of the sort in it. If, however, such incidents are unavoidable, they should be outside the piece, like the hero's ignorance in Oedipus of the circumstances of Lams' death; not within it, like the report of the Pythian games in Electra, or the man's having come to Mysia from Tegea without uttering a word on the way, in The Mysians.

So that it is ridiculous to say that one's Plot would have been spoilt without them, since it is fundamentally wrong to make up such Plots. If the poet has taken such a Plot, however, and one sees that he might have put it in a more probable form, he is guilty of absurdity as well as a fault of art. Even in the Odyssey the improbabilities in the setting-ashore of Ulysses would be clearly intolerable in the hands of an inferior poet. As it is, the poet conceals them, his other excellences veiling their absurdity. Elaborate Diction, however, is required only in places where there is no action, and no Character or Thought to be revealed.

Where there is Character or Thought, on the other hand, an over-ornate Diction tends to obscure them. As regards Problems and their Solutions, one may see the number and nature of the assumptions on which they proceed by viewing the matter in the following way. The poet being an imitator just like the painter or other maker of likenesses, he must necessarily in all instances represent things in one or other of three aspects, either as they were or are, or as they are said or thought to be or to have been, or as they ought to be. All this he does in language, with an admixture, it may be, of strange words and metaphors, as also of the various modified forms of words, since the use of these is conceded in poetry. It is to be remembered, too, that there is not the same kind of correctness in poetry as in politics, or indeed any other art. There is, however, within the limits of poetry itself a possibility of two kinds of error, the one directly, the other only accidentally connected with the art.

If the poet meant to describe the thing correctly, and failed through lack of power of expression, his art itself is at fault. But if it was through his having meant to describe it in some incorrect way (e.g. to make the horse in movement have both right legs thrown forward) that the technical error (one in a matter of, say, medicine or some other special science), or impossibilities of whatever kind they may be, have got into his description, hi.e.ror in that case is not in the essentials of the poetic art. These, therefore, must be the premisses of the Solutions in answer to the criticisms involved in the Problems.

- As to the criticisms relating to the poet's art itself. Any impossibilities there may be in his descriptions of things are faults. But from another point of view they are justifiable, if they serve the end of poetry itself—if (to assume what we have said of that end) they make the effect of some portion of the work more astounding. The Pursuit of Hector is an instance in point. If, however, the poetic end might have been as well or better attained without sacrifice of technical correctness in such matters, the impossibility is not to be justified, since the description should be, if it can, entirely free from error. One may ask, too, whether the error is in a matter directly or only accidentally connected with the poetic art; since it is a lesser error in an artist not to know, for instance, that the hind has no horns, than to produce an unrecognizable picture of one.
- If the poet's description be criticized as not true to fact, one may urge perhaps that the object ought to be as described—an answer like that of Sophocles, who said that he drew men as they ought to be, and Euripides as they were. If the description, however, be neither true nor of the thing as it ought to be, the answer must be then, that it is in accordance with opinion. The tales about Gods, for instance, may be as wrong as Xenophanes thinks, neither true nor the better thing to say; but they are certainly in accordance with opinion. Of other statements in poetry one may perhaps say, not that they are better than the truth, but that the fact was so at the time; e.g. the description of the arms: 'their spears stood upright, butt-end upon the ground'; for that was the

usual way of fixing them then, as it is still with the Illyrians. As for the question whether something said or done in a poem is morally right or not, in dealing with that one should consider not only the intrinsic quality of the actual word or deed, but also the person who says or does it, the person to whom he says or does it, the time, the means, and the motive of the agent—whether he does it to attain a greate.g.od, or to avoid a greater evil.)

- Other criticisms one must meet by considering the language of the poet:
  - by the assumption of a strange word in a passage like oureas men proton, where by oureas Homer may perhaps mean not mules but sentinels. And in saying of Dolon, hos p e toi eidos men heen kakos, his meaning may perhaps be, not that Dolon's body was deformed, but that his face was ugly, as eneidos is the Cretan word for handsome-faced. So, too, goroteron de keraie may mean not 'mix the wine stronger', as though for topers, but 'mix it quicker'.
  - Other expressions in Homer may be explained as metaphorical; e.g. in halloi men ra theoi te kai aneres eudon (hapantes) pannux as compared with what he tells us at the same time, e toi hot hes pedion to Troikon hathreseien, aulon suriggon *te homadon* the word hapantes 'all', is metaphorically put for 'many', since 'all' is a species of 'many '. So also his oie d' ammoros is metaphorical, the best known standing 'alone'.
  - A change, as Hippias suggested, in the mode of reading a word will solve the difficulty in didomen de oi, and to men ou kataputhetai hombro.
  - Other difficulties may be solved by another punctuation; e.g. in Empedocles, aipsa de thnet ephyonto, ta prin mathon athanata xora te prin kekreto.

Or

— by the assumption of an equivocal term, as in parocheken de pleo nux, where pleo i.e.uivocal.

Or

— by an appeal to the custom of language. Wine-and-water we call 'wine'; and it is on the same principle that Homer speaks of a knemis neoteuktou kassiteroio, a 'greave of new-wrought tin.'

A worker in iron we call a 'brazier'; and it is on the same principle that Ganymede is described as the 'wine-server' of Zeus, though the Gods do not drink wine. This latter, however, may be an instance of metaphor.

But whenever also a word seems to imply some contradiction, it is necessary to reflect how many ways there may be of understanding it in the passage in question; e.g. in Homer's te r' hesxeto xalkeon hegxos one should consider the possible senses of 'was stopped there'—whether by taking it in this sense or in that one will best avoid the fault of which Glaucon speaks:

'They start with some improbable presumption; and having so decreed it themselves, proceed to draw inferences, and censure the poet as though he had actually said whatever they happen to believe, if his statement conflicts with their own notion of things.' This is how Homer's silence about Icarius has been treated.

Starting with, the notion of his having been a Lacedaemonian, the critics think it strange for Telemachus not to have met him when he went to Lacedaemon. Whereas the fact may have been as the Cephallenians say, that the wife of Ulysses was of a Cephallenian family, and that her father's name was Icadius, not Icarius. So that it is probably a mistake of the critics that has given rise to the Problem.

Speaking generally, one has to justify

- The Impossible by reference to the requirements of poetry, or to the better, or to opinion. For the purposes of poetry a convincing impossibility is preferable to an unconvincing possibility; and if men such as Zeuxis depicted be impossible, the answer is that it is better they should be like that, as the artist ought to improve on his model.

- The Improbable one has to justify either by showing it to be in accordance with opinion, or by urging that at times it is not improbable; for there is a probability of things happening also against probability.
- The contradictions found in the poet's language one should first test as one does an opponent's confutation in a dialectical argument, so as to see whether he means the same thing, in the same relation, and in the same sense, before admitting that he has contradicted either something he has said himself or what a man of sound sense assumes as true. But there is no possible apology for improbability of Plot or depravity of character, when they are not necessary and no use is made of them, like the improbability in the appearance of Aegeus in Medea and the baseness of Menelaus in Orestes.

The objections, then, of critics start with faults of five kinds: the allegation is always that something i.e.ther (1) impossible, (2) improbable, (3) corrupting, (4) contradictory, or (5) against technical correctness. The answers to these objections must be sought under one or other of the above-mentioned heads, which are twelve in number.

The question may be raised whether the epic or the tragic is the higher form of imitation. It may be argued that, if the less vulgar is the higher, and the less vulgar is always that which addresses the better public, an art addressing any and every one is of a very vulgar order. It is a belief that their public cannot see the meaning, unless they add something themselves, that causes the perpetual movements of the performers—bad flute-players, for instance, rolling about, if quoit-throwing is to be represented, and pulling at the conductor, if Scylla is the subject of the piece. Tragedy, then, is said to be an art of this order—to be in fact just what the later actors were in the eyes of their predecessors; for Myrmiscus used to call Callippides 'the ape', because he thought he so overacted his parts; and a similar view was taken of Pindarus also. All Tragedy, however, is said to stand to the Epic as the newer to the older school of actors.

The one, accordingly, is said to address a cultivated 'audience, which does not need the accompaniment of gesture; the other, an uncultivated one. If, therefore, Tragedy is a vulgar art, it must clearly be lower than the Epic. The answer to this is twofold. In the first place, one may urge

- That the censure does not touch the art of the dramatic poet, but only that of his interpreter; for it is quite possible to overdo the gesturing even in an epic recital, as did Sosistratus, and in a singing contest, as did Mnasitheus of Opus.
- That one should not condemn all movement, unless one means to condemn even the dance, but only that of ignoble people—which is the point of the criticism passed on Callippides and in the present day on others, that their women are not like gentlewomen.
- That Tragedy may produce its effect even without movement or action in just the same way as Epic poetry; for from the mere reading of a play its quality may be seen. So that, if it be superior in all other respects, thi.e.ement of inferiority is not a necessary part of it.

In the second place, one must remember

- That Tragedy has everything that the Epic has (even the epic meter being admissible), together with a not inconsiderable addition in the shape of the Music (a very real factor in the pleasure of the drama) and the Spectacle.
- That its reality of presentation is felt in the play as read, as well as in the play as acted.
- That the tragic imitation requires less space for the attainment of its end; which is a great advantage, since the more concentrated effect is more pleasurable than one with a large admixture of time to dilute it—consider the Oedipus of Sophocles, for instance, and the effect of expanding it into the number of lines of the Iliad.

- That there is less unity in the imitation of the epic poets, as is proved by the fact that any one work of theirs supplies matter for several tragedies; the result being that, if they take what is really a single story, it seems curt when briefly told, and thin and waterish when on the scale of length usual with their verse. In saying that there is less unity in an epic, I mean an epic made up of a plurality of actions, in the same way as the Iliad and Odyssey have many such parts, each one of them in itself of some magnitude; yet the structure of the two Homeric poems is as perfect as can be, and the action in them is as nearly as possible one action.

If, then, Tragedy is superior in these respects, and also besides these, in its poeti.e.fect (since the two forms of poetry should give us, not any or every pleasure, but the very special kind we have mentioned), it is clear that, as attaining the poeti.e.fect better than the Epic, it will be the higher form of art. So much for Tragedy and Epic poetry—for these two arts in general and their species; the number and nature of their constituent parts; the causes of success and failure in them; the Objections of the critics, and the Solutions in answer to them.

Chapter 15

Summary an Analysis

Summary and Analysis of Chapters 1-5

Summary

Aristotle begins with a loose outline of what he will address in The Poetics:

- The different kinds of poetry and the 'essential quality' of each
- The structure necessary for a 'good poem'
- The method in which a poem is divided into parts
- Anything else that might tangentially comes up in his address of the above topics.

But before he begins tackling these topics, Aristotle first seeks to define poetry. Poetry, as Aristotle defines it, is first and foremost a 'medium of imitation,' meaning a form of art that seeks to duplicate or represent life. Poetry can imitate life in a number of ways, by representing character, emotion, action, or even everyday objects.

Poetry, as Aristotle defines it, includes epic poetry, tragedy, comedy, dithyrambic poetry, and music (specifically of flute, and lyre). What differentiates these kinds of poetry is the nature of their 'imitation.' He notes three differences.

Medium of Imitation

In general, poetry imitates life through rhythm, language, and harmony. This is more pronounced in music or dance, but even verse poetry can accomplish imitation through language alone

Object of Imitation

Art seeks to imitate men in action - hence the term 'drama' (dramitas, in Greek). In order to imitate men, art must either present man as 'better' than they are in life (i.e. of higher morals), as true to life, or as 'worse' than they are in life (i.e. of lower morals).

Each author has his own tendencies - Homer 'makes mèn better than they are,' Cleophon 'as they are', Nichochares 'worse than they are.' But more important is a general distinction that Aristotle makes between forms of drama: comedy represents men as worse then they are, tragedy as better than they are in actual life.

- Mode of Imitation
  A poet can imitate either through:
- Narration, in which he takes another personality (an omniscient 'I' watching the events 'like an observer')
- Speak in his own person, unchanged (the first-person 'I')
- Presents all his characters as living and moving before us (third-person narrator)

Continuing on from imitation, Aristotle turns to the anthropology and history of poetry. As Aristotle sees it, poetry emerged for two reasons 1) man's instinct to imitate things and 2) the instinct for 'harmony' and rhythm.

Once poetry emerged, it evolved in two directions. One group of poems imitated 'noble actions,' or the actions of good men. A second group of poets imitated 'the actions of meaner persons' in the form of satire. The former evolved into tragedy, the latter into epic poetry, then tragic drama.

Tragedy began as improvisation and evolved over time, through the contribution of Aeschylus, Sophocles, and others into its natural form of dramatic plot, dialogue, and iambic verse. Comedy began as an imitation of characters 'of a lower type', meaning a representation of a defect or ugliness in character, which is not painful or destructive. Comedy was at first not taken seriously, but once plot was introduced in Sicily comedic theater, it soon grew into a respected form.

Epic poetry, finally, imitates men of noble action, like tragedy. But epic poetry only allows one kind of meter and is narrative in form. Moreover, tragedy usually confines itself to a single day, whereas epic poetry has no limits of time. Ultimately, all the elements of an epic poem are found in tragedy, but not all the elements of tragedy are found in an epic poem.

Analysis

The Poetics begins quickly and efficiently, unlike a number of Aristotle's other works. Instead of laying out an argument for why the subjects merits such a discussion or an overall thesis for his investigation, he immediately lays out an outline for his work - types of poetry, structure, and division - and begins his systematic analysis.

As one critic notes, "The preliminaries are over in ten lines... Nothing is said about the purpose of the discussion, what Aristotle hopes to accomplish by it; next to nothing about method, or the views of others on poetry. But above all we miss something that stands as preface to every major work of Aristotle's [best work], namely some general statement by way of orientation..." (Else, 2). In other words, Aristotle usually presents a 'notion of the forest,' before he begins to look at the trees. But not in the Poetics.

The first three chapters of the Poetics are action-packed - nearly every line needs to be carefully dealt with, since Aristotle presents a myriad of definitions, concepts, and categories. But the first major issue is to understand involves the term 'Poetics' - what does Aristotle mean by it? Simply put, 'poetry' to Aristotle is not the final product, but the art of creating poetry. To understand this art, we must first grasp a number of important concepts.

The first is 'imitation,' which is a word used often in the Poetics. 'Imitation,' as a concept, refers to an artist's primary motivation to duplicate or capture life in some form. Imitation, furthermore, is an innate instinct, says Aristotle, that is 'implanted in man from childhood.' We use imitation not only for entertainment, but also for learning - by seeing the fortunes or misfortunes of another, they can internalize experience through vicarious living.

Aristotle also uses imitation to differentiate between tragedy and comedy. In the former, poets reveal men as better than they are - hence the tragic 'hero.' It is in this representation of man as 'better' or of 'higher morality' that we ultimately find catharsis, the release at the end of a tragedy.

In comedy, however, a poet presents man as worse than he is - plagued by some defect or ugliness which ultimately takes the reader into a satiric worldview. Comedy ultimately works in a similar way to tragedy, but with opposite effect: in a tragedy, we grieve over the fate of a man who must suffer for his flaw, perhaps touched by the possibility that we too might possess this flaw. But in a comedy, we laugh at the hero's flaw, comforted by the fact that it is not ours.

Indeed, comedy and tragedy both have a moralizing effect on the audience. This is less evident in comedy, perhaps, since "comedies tend to be about bad behaviour and people doing ugly, immoral, or ridiculous things."

The critic Goucher explains how Aristotle solves this problem: "[Aristotle] accepted that the primary object of comedy as imitation: imitation of low characters - not morally bad, but ludicrous, ugly but not painful or destructive. He defended comedies' mimetic representation of ludicrous behaviour because it would incite audiences to avoid its imitation" (Goucher 1).

Aristotle's definition of epic poetry may confuse the reader, so it is worth illuminating precisely what he means. Epic poetry is like tragedy in that it reveals man to be better than he is - but it is narrative in form, depending either on an omniscient first-person narrator, a third-person narrator, or a first-person narrating hero.

A tragedy, meanwhile, involves the dialogue of two or more characters. Additionally, tragedy and epic poetry differ in length — tragedy is confined usually to a single day, in the efforts to reveal a quick devolution of the hero. Epic poetry, meanwhile, often continues for a man's full lifetime. Ultimately it seems that tragedy grew from epic poetry, so we find all the qualities of the latter in the former, but an epic poem need not contain all the elements of a tragedy.

Summary and Analysis of Chapters 6-9

Summary

Tragedy is an imitation of action with the following characteristics: it is serious, complete, of significant magnitude, depicted with rhythmic language and/or song, in the form of action (not narrative), and produces a 'purgation' of pity and fear in the audience (also known as catharsis).

Since tragedy is the imitation of action, it is chiefly concerned with the lives of men, and thus presents a stage for character and thought. Character - the qualities ascribed to a certain man - and thought, according to Aristotle, are the two causes from which actions spring. These elements also determine the success of a given action. Plot, then, is arrangements of incidents (successes or failures) that result from character and thought giving way to action.

With the above in mind, Aristotle lays out the six parts that define a tragedy:

- Plot
- Character
- Diction (rhythmic language)
- Thought
- Spectacle
- Song

Plot is the most important part of a tragedy for a number of reasons. First, the result of a man's actions determines his success or failure, and hence his happiness, so it is action which is paramount - not character, which doesn't necessarily affect every action. Second, without action, there cannot be a tragedy - but there can be a tragedy without character. Thirdly, diction, song, and thought - even elegantly combined - cannot replicate the action of life without plot.

Plot, then, is the 'soul of a tragedy,' and character comes second. Rounding out his rankings: thought, meaning what a character says in a given circumstance, followed by diction, song, and spectacle.

Aristotle goes on to describe the elements of plot, which include completeness, magnitude, unity, determinate structure, and universality. Completeness refers to the necessity of a tragedy to have a beginning, middle, and end. A 'beginning' is defined as an origin, by which something naturally comes to be.

An 'end,' meanwhile, follows another incident by necessity, but has nothing necessarily following it. The 'middle' follows something just as something must follow it. 'Magnitude' refers simply to length — the tragedy must be of a 'length which can be easily embraced by the memory.' That said, Aristotle believes that the longer a tragedy, the more beautiful it can be, provided it maintains its beginning, middle, and end. And in the sequence of these three acts, the tragedy will present a change 'from bad fortune to good, or from good fortune to bad.'

'Unity' refers to the centering of all the plot's action around a common theme or idea. 'Determinate structure' refers to the fact that the plot all hinges on a sequence of causal, imitative events, so if one were to remove even one part of the plot, the entire tragedy 'will be disjointed and disturbed.' More simply, every part of a good plot is necessary. 'Universality' refers to the necessity of a given character to speak or act according to how all or most humans would react in a given situation, 'according to the law of probability or necessity.'

Aristotle ends this discussion of plot elements by pointing his out his particular disdain for 'episodic' plots - plots in which episodes succeed one another 'without probably or necessary sequence' (like a weekly sitcom, for instance). These episodic dramas stretch plot 'beyond their capacity,' and hence are inorganic.

Analysis

Aristotle highlights the primacy of action in this section as the key to an artist's imitation. Indeed, because action initiates a chain of causal events, it is the single most important driver of plot. Though an astute reader might ask 'But what causes action?', Aristotle quickly responds by arguing that ultimately the things that drive action - character and thought - aren't nearly as important as the action itself. For plot is the simple arrangement of incidents in causal chains, and in this plot alone we can find satisfaction, even if it is not clearly motivated with character or thought.

That said, the best of tragedies maintain the primacy of plot while also inlaying the drama with character, diction (rhythmic language), thought, spectacle, and song. Character here refers to the attributes either ascribed or clearly evident in a given man - virtues which ultimately define a tragic hero's flaw and the source of his redemption. Thought, meanwhile, refers to the ideas of a given character, conveyed by speech.

Though thought illuminates character, it is not necessary for it - indeed, a silent hero still would have a clearly delineated character, and perhaps an even clearer one than a loquacious character. Again, Aristotle's thesis is proved - that it is action that is paramount, regardless of motivation or underlying cause.

'Unity' is another concept which may confuse the reader, since Aristotle does not spend much time explicating it. Unity refers to the ability of the best plots to revolve around an axis, a theme which 'unites' all the action. A unified drama will have a 'spine' - a central idea which motivates all the action, characters, thoughts, diction, and spectacle. 'Determinate structure' follows from unity — if the action revolves around a central spine, it creates a full skeleton of plot. But remove one bone, and the entire body of action becomes unstable, since every bone radiates from the central spine and is thus fully necessary. The test, Aristotle says, is to see if there is any part of the plot which can be removed without missing it. If this is true, then it must be excised. A true drama never wanders from its central spine for fear of losing its unity.

'Universality', meanwhile, is slightly more vague, but appeals to our common sense. Aristotle simply states that a character must act in accordance with human nature - either through probability, i.e. what 'most of us' would do, or through necessity, i.e. what we are 'forced' to do. An action cannot seem arbitrary - otherwise not only will it violate the determinate structure and break unity, but it will also irritate an audience that sees no basis for the action in human behaviour.

Summary and Analysis of Chapters 10-12

Summary

In order for plot to function, it not only needs the basic concepts from the previous chapters, but the following components as well: astonishment, reversal (or peripeteia), recognition, and suffering. Astonishment refers to a tragedy's ability to inspire 'fear and pity.' Both fear and pity are elicited from an audience when the events come by surprise, but not by chance. The surprise that drives the tragedy must feel like it is part of a grander design. Reversal is the change by which the main action of the story comes full-circle — for example, In Oedipus, the messenger who comes to free Oedipus from his fears of his mother produces the opposite effect with his news. Recognition is the change from ignorance to knowledge, usually involving people coming to understand the identities of one another or discovering whether a person 'has done a thing or not.' The best forms of recognition are linked with a reversal (as in Oedipus) and, in tandem, will produce pity and fear from the audience. Suffering is a destructive or painful action, which is often the result of a reversal or recognition. Aristotle points out that a 'simple' plot omits a reversal or recognition, but a 'complex plot has one or the other - or both, if it is truly transcendent.

All tragedies, however, depend on suffering as part of its attempt to elicit pity and fear from the audience. Finally, Aristotle points out the structural parts of a tragedy (or 'quantitative' parts, as he calls them). These are the prologue, episode, exode, and choric song. The prologue is the part of the tragedy which precedes the first undivided utterance of the chorus. The episode is the part of the tragedy between choral songs, and the exode is the first part of a tragedy with no choric song after it.

Analysis

Three key concepts are introduced in this section - reversal, recognition, and catharsis (though Aristotle refers to the last as 'purgation.') A simple tragedy will have none of these elements (or a perfunctory catharsis), but a complex tragedy will use reversal and recognition to achieve catharsis.

Reversal works in tandem with a story's spine or centre to ensure that the hero comes full circle. Oedipus is the best example of a hero who encounters such a reversal — he hears news that his fears have been allayed, the mystery solved, and then in the course of enjoying this relief and hearing the news, he realizes that it in fact implicates him. Often, recognition is a tool to achieve this reversal or a byproduct of it — in this case, Oedipus recognizes the true identity of his father and mother, the nature of his own crimes, and the accuracy of the prophecy.

In one swift blow, Oedipus has come full circle and is now the victim of his own search for justice and truth. The concept of suffering is slightly misleading in that it does not refer simply to a character's endurance of physical and emotional pain. In order to truly produce catharsis - the commingling of fear and pity in an audience - the suffering must be a consequence of reversal or recognition.

And indeed, the more surprising the reversal or recognition - as in the case of Oedipus - the more the audience will themselves suffer empathetically, realizing that they too have been ambushed by the causal chain of the plot. Even as 'objective' observers, audience members too are flawed - and thus learn from the tragic hero's fate.

Catharsis, then, is pity for the hero, and fear that his fate could befall us. While pity is the result of any combination of reversal and recognition, fear can only be a product of reversal and recognition crafted into a surprising ending to the plot. And indeed, the absolute pinnacle of tragedy comes when surprise, reversal, recognition, and suffering are united around the core spine of the story in a swift blow to the audience at the end of the third act.

Summary and Analysis of Chapters 13-16

Summary

Aristotle next addresses what elements comprise the 'best' tragic plots. First, a perfect tragedy should have a complex plan - thus using reversal and recognition to imitate actions which elicit fear or pity in the audience. And yet, a good tragedy does not simply present the spectacle of a virtuous man suffering adversity, for that is merely 'shocking' and does not make us empathize with the hero.

If pity is aroused by 'unmerited misfortune,' and fear by 'the misfortune of a man like ourselves,' then a good tragedy presents a character whose downfall comes because of a flaw in him-'an error or frailty.' Though he is renowned, prosperous, even seeming virtuous, there is a chink in his armor that will inevitably be found - and will be the source of his demise. Fear and pity truly can only be elicited through this tragic flaw in the hero which in turn is motivated by the 'unity' or spine of the entire piece. Some poets, says Aristotle, use spectacle to motivate fear and pity, but this ultimately does not resonate for long, since spectacle produces a different type of 'pleasure' than the one requisite for tragedy. Only pity and fear can produce true 'purgation' or emotions, rather than a spectacle of false catharsis. Aristotle next summarizes the circumstances that make for good tragedy. First, it must involve incidents between people who are 'dear to one another' - i.e. a son killing a mother, a brother killing a brother, etc. There are all kinds of permutations of such an incident:

- The act can be done consciously and with knowledge of the people involved (i.e. Medea slaying her children)
- The act can be done ignorantly, and the tie of family or friendship discovered afterwards (i.e. Oedipus)
- The act is not done, because the hero can't go through with it
- The act is about to be done, but then the discovery reveals the true identities of the characters, and the deed is stopped before it does irreparable harm.

Aristotle points out that case c) is the least dramatic (though it works in Antigone), and that d) is likely the most effective.

When it comes to character, a poet should aim for four things. First, the hero must be 'good,' and thus manifest moral purpose in his speech. Second, the hero must have propriety, or 'manly valor.' Thirdly, the hero must be 'true to life.' And finally, the hero must be consistent.

The concept of 'true to life' is addressed further, and Aristotle points out that a well-drawn character acts out of 'probability and necessity,' not because of some arbitrary traits bestowed upon him by the author. Moreover, the unraveling of the plot comes from the actions of the plot itself - the inner logic of the chain of events, rather than the character himself. Indeed, a well-drawn character is simply in service of the plot.

Aristotle next lists the types of recognition available to a poet. First, there is recognition by signs - bodily marks, external ornaments like jewelry, or some other marking that delineates the secret identity of a person. Aristotle calls this type of recognition the 'least artistic type.'

Second, there is recognition 'invented by will,' or the sudden revelation of an identity without forewarning or necessity. This too, says Aristotle, is a type of device 'wanting in art.'

A third type is recognition from memory, where a character sees an object and it 'awakens a feeling,' and recognition from 'reasoning' provides a fourth type, where the character determines a secret identity through a process of deduction. Fifth is recognition involving 'false interference,' where a messenger or outside character facilitates the revelation.

But the sixth and best type of recognition is one that 'arises from the incidents themselves' and the discovery is made naturally in the course of the plot. Again, Aristotle points to Oedipus Rex as the model, since nothing in the construction of the revelation is artificial. It is simply a process of the plot's unravelling from the centre, an essential core of the drama's unity.

Analysis

Aristotle underscores the significance of recognition in this section, as a crucial element in producing tragic catharsis. As in other chapters of The Poetics, he creates a hierarchy of tools available to a poet in order to point out which type of recognition is 'best.'

Recognition by 'signs', though mocked by Aristotle, is clearly the most familiar to modern audiences. Indeed, most contemporary thrillers involve the discovery of a sign in the climactic 'twist' - either a marking on a victim's body, a hidden piece of jewelry, etc. (The Silence of the Lambs, for instance, depends on Clarice's discovery of a sign in the killer's house.)

Recognition by 'invention' might seem vague, but again it is a device that reappears often in contemporary work. In Seven, for instance, the villainous character, played by Kevin Spacey, has to announce the impending recognition so that the hero and audience can react - something that Aristotle, no doubt, would scorn, since it produces only fleeting pity and fear.

The best type of recognition arises when the entire narrative revolves around the given revelation - when it is an inevitable result of the beginning incident, even though the audience does not know it as such. A good contemporary example might be Alfred Hitchcock's Psycho, where the source of evil becomes clearer and clearer as the movie evolves - but never so clear enough that we can determine what it is until it is too late.

Remember that ultimately all these elements are leading towards catharsis - and it is the effectiveness of catharsis that demonstrates the power of the particular dramatic work. Catharsis may seem like a vague emotional construct, but it is a product of very deliberate plot choices (i.e. reversal and recognition.) As one critic notes, "If catharsis has anything to do with the emotional side of tragedy - and we cannot doubt that it has - then it, like the tragic emotions and the tragic pleasure, must be 'built into' the plot and thus made available to a reader in the same way, on the same terms, as it is to the spectator in the theater".

It is also significant to note Aristotle's delineation of the tragic hero's character. The tragic hero is not an eminently 'good' man, or model of virtue swiftly brought down by adversity. In that, says Aristotle, there is only shock - since we can see none of ourselves in a perfectly virtuous man, and find it arbitrary that he would be selected for cosmic punishment. What is far more effective is if the hero possesses some 'frailty', or flaw (like Achilles' heel), which he compensates for, hides, runs away from - but eventually catches up with him. An 'error' of character should not be confused with an error in a character's 'action' - a tragedy must spin on a fundamental flaw in the hero's behaviour and one that the audience can identify with or substitute in themselves. Only through the tragic climax can he - and the audience - find redemption.

Summary and Analysis of Chapters 17-20

Summary

Aristotle points out that visualizing the action is crucial for a poet in order to avoid gaps in logic or inconsistencies. Rather than see the action in his head, Aristotle says the poet must work out the action 'before his eyes.'

Aristotle also suggests that a poet construct a general outline and then fill in episodes and detail. Thus, a poet can work out a play's essence, and then focus on the episodes that will support this essence and in effect, create 'unity.'

Every tragedy contains two parts - complication and unraveling (denouement). The complication refers to everything from the beginning of the action to the turning point, or climax where bad fortune turns to good, or good fortune turns to bad. The unraveling, or denouement, extends from the climax to the end, and tracks the final transformation of a hero to good or bad fortune.

Aristotle presents four kinds of tragedy:

- *Complex:* depending entirely on reversal and recognition at the climax
- *Pathetic:* motivated by passion

- *Ethical:* motivated by moral purpose
- *Simple:* without reversal or recognition

Aristotle concludes his discussion of reversal and recognition by suggesting that a tragedy should not assume an epic structure - involving many plots. One plot that creates unity of action is all that is required for tragic catharsis.

Aristotle moves on to diction next, or the expression of thought through speech. Speech can be divided into a) proof and refutation, b) excitation of feelings (pity, fear, and anger), or c) the suggestion of importance. Indeed, action can be divided similarly-but the difference between action and speech is that action can stand alone without exposition, while speech depends on the effect of the speech in order to gain a result. The speech, in itself, is an action.

Analysis

Aristotle begins here with an important note on visualization. Whereas even many contemporary authors and instructors focus on the value of seeing the action 'in your head,' Aristotle points out that such methods inevitably lead to gaps in logic and inconsistencies, since the action is being conjured by an unreliable mind. Rather, the best way to determine whether the action of a given drama can sustain audience's interest and believability is by envisioning it 'before one's eyes' as if unfolding in a proscenium before the writer. As such, the writer becomes objective observer of the action and can immediately point out what does not follow from probable or necessary cause.

There are only two parts to a drama, says Aristotle - the complication and the denouement. More simply, the complication begins with an 'inciting incident,' a trigger that puts a chain of events in motion.

At some point the chain reaches a climax, where the hero's fortunes must irreversibly turn from good to bad (a tragedy) or bad to good (a comedy). The denouement (or unraveling) is simply the end of this transformation that begins at the climax.

For instance, in Oedipus Rex, the complication sees us all

the way through Oedipus discovering his own crimes - and from there, the denouement takes us through his self-mutilation and redemption. Often, then, the climax takes place at the moment of key reversal or recognition in a tragedy. Without this reversal or recognition, the author must rely on some other form of invention in order to create a climax - either 'ethics' or 'passion' as Aristotle states in his summary of the types of tragedy, or a purposeful 'simplicity' to the drama.

Aristotle's definition of 'diction' is revelatory even in contemporary academic circles, because it subjugates speech to action without condition. For Aristotle, action is always paramount - even without speech at all, one could create a perfectly sustainable, even masterful drama. Speech, then, must be seen as an action in itself and not a complement to action.

Indeed, the best speech has the same purpose as action - to either prove or refute, incite fear or pity, or suggest significance. The last is where speech might prove more useful than physical action in most cases - since the highlighting of a particular object or character can be done more simply with words than with the limitations of staging. That said, one can also point to film as a genre where suggesting significance is nearly always done without words - the shot of the gun in the drawer, for instance, nearly always tells us that the gun will reappear at the climax of the film. Ultimately, then, speech must simply do what action can accomplish with less effort - which is to direct the audience's attention to a given purpose, emotion, or significance.

Summary and Analysis of Chapters 21-24

Summary

Aristotle classifies Greek words in an esoteric discussion of 'simple' and 'compound' terms, and the reader can sift through a majority of this analysis and focus instead on his definition of a few key literary terms.

First is 'metaphor,' or the use of 'transference' to link two unlike things. 'Life's setting sun,' for instance, does not hedge or qualify its comparison with 'like' or 'as' (that would be a simile), or create primacy around one term (as in an analogy). Instead, a metaphor simply links two objects with the understanding that the reader will find the unity of concept that connects them.

Aristotle points out that the best poetry uses only 'current and proper words,' meaning the contemporary lexicon. When an author resorts to 'lofty' or esoteric language, he alienates the reader. Indeed, a metaphor, says Aristotle, only truly works when it uses ordinary words; if one were to use 'strange' or 'raised' words for a metaphor or other literary device, it simply collapses into jargon.

And yet, Aristotle also permits the good poet to lengthen, contract, and alter words to fit his purpose. By playing with ordinary words, the poet creates 'distinct' language, but at the same time ensures that the reader will maintain clarity. By playing with accepted or ordinary words, the poet can engage the reader at the highest level. (One can think of Shakespeare here, and the way he so often uses recognizable words in extraordinary ways to achieve his rhythms and images.)

Aristotle next proceeds to a discussion of the epic form - which employs a single meter, a dramatic plot, unity, and all the other features of a tragedy. (As mentioned before, a proper epic maintains all the elements of a tragedy, since tragedy evolved from the epic form.) An epic does not portray a single action, but rather a single 'period,' thus often charting the course of many characters over the course of many events.

Epic poetry falls into the same categories as tragedy: simple, complex, ethical or pathetic. Also like tragedy, it requires reversals, recognitions, scenes of suffering, and artistic thought and diction. There are a few differences between tragedy and epic, however. First, an epic poem, however, will not use song or spectacle to achieve its cathartic effect. Second, epics often cannot be presented at a single sitting, whereas tragedies are usually capable of being brought within a single view. Epic poetry, after all, is not confined to the stage - and thus, many events and characters can be presented simultaneously because of its narrative form.

Finally, the 'heroic measure' of epic poetry is hexameter, where tragedy often uses other forms of meter to achieve the rhythms of different characters' speech.

Aristotle points out that the poet should take as little part as possible in the actual story of an epic - meaning limited first-person narration, and no personal appearances in scenes if possible. At the same time, 'wonderment,' created by absurdity or irrational events for the purposes of indulging the reader's pleasure, is allowed in an epic poem - even moreso than in a tragedy. An absurd event or moment can pass more unnoticed in an epic poem, simply because it is not being dramatized onstage.

That said, Aristotle notes that a tragic plot cannot have 'irrational parts.' There must be likelihood, no matter how seemingly impossible the circumstances - as long as we trust that given the initial incident, the plot follows logically and probably, then the poet is in the realm of good drama. But if we believe neither the inciting incident, nor the chain of events that follows, the poem is simply absurd, and thus summarily dismissed.

Analysis

Chapters 21 and 22 of The Poetics offer a complex discussion of language types and tropes that a reader unversed in the scripts of ancient Greek can quickly sift through. He does, however, stop to offer a clear and concise discussion of the use of metaphor - a device of figurative language that is frequently misunderstood.

A metaphor is not simply a comparison of objects - but rather the use of two unlike things in proximity in order to illustrate a larger, unified concept. The second term in the metaphor, then, is subsumed by the first - in the case, for instance, of 'life's setting sun,' the sun becomes part of a fictional trope illustrating the ebb and flow of life. A good metaphor forces us to actually position the objects together in an imaginary, but completely probable relationship. And furthermore, a metaphor - unlike a simile or analogy, which establishes the primacy of the first term can easily be reversed.

After hearing the metaphor of 'life's setting sun,' we can then look at the sun and see in its rise and fall the course of life. Metaphors, then, are more fluid than the rest of figurative language, and hence Aristotle focuses on them as the primary device of the good poet.

Metaphor also replicates the human instinct to find connections through imitation. As one critic notes, "The metaphorical system of the myth imitates life with the organization of metaphors and the story line. Metaphors imitate it statically and the story dynamically". As Aristotle pointed out earlier in the Poetics, we cannot help but imitate as a device for learning.

The metaphor offers the clearest device for imitation while also maintaining enough idiosyncrasy for the author to engage the reader in his own imaginative world. The difference between epic poetry and tragedy may confuse some readers, but it can be boiled down simply to the fact that epic poetry unfolds in a narrative form, as in the Iliad, while a tragedy depends on staging for its cathartic effect (Oedipus).

The brief distinction that Aristotle makes between the two forms on the basis of spectacle has wider implications, perhaps, then he gives it. Epic poetry has no need for spectacle because it gains its design from a large span of time. Tragedy, however, is limited in its time frame - usually to a single day - and thus the spectacle of suffering and horror is necessary for catharsis.

Finally, Aristotle points out that despite the invention required for tragedy and epic, both forms depend on likelihood and probability. A tragedy depends on probability even more than the epic, in that the events are dramatized, forcing us to filter all the events onstage through our own experience and classify it as either 'rational' or 'absurd.' An epic poem, however, has more room for maneuvering, since the oral tradition allows a balancing of the irrational with the pleasures of indulgence as long as the reader can imagine some world where the fiction could be real, then he will continue to find the story engaging. If, however, he finds that the action is 'false,' then the causal chain of plot is broken, and often the work can never recover.

Summary and Analysis of Chapters 25-26

Summary

Aristotle next tackles 'critical difficulties' that a poet may face and the solutions that will ensure his success. He names three major 'solutions' for poets in attempting to imitate action and life:

- The poet must imitate either things as they are, things as they are thought to be, or things as they ought to be
- The poet must imitate in action and language; the latter must be current terms, or metaphors (and occasionally rare words)
- Errors come when the poet imitates incorrectly - and thus destroys the essence of the poem - or when the poet accidentally makes an error (a factual error, for instance), which does not ultimately sabotage the entire work. The only error that matters is one that touches the essential of the given work - for instance, 'not to know that a hind has no horns is a less serious matter than to paint it inartistically.'

Critics often argue with a poet's work if it is seen as either impossible, irrational, morally hurtful, contradictory, or contrary to artistic correctness. Aristotle refutes all of these judgments by saying simply that it is the purpose - the essence - of the work that matters, and its goal in imitating reality as it is, as it is thought to be, or as it ought to be.

Aristotle concludes by tackling the question of whether the epic or tragic form is 'the higher.' Most critics of his time argued that tragedy was for an inferior audience that required the gesture of performers, while epic poetry was for a 'cultivated audience' which could filter a narrative form through their own imagined characters.

Aristotle replies with the following:

- Epic recitation can be marred with overdone gesticulation in the same way as a tragedy; there is no guarantee that the epic form is not one motivated by the oral gestures of the ones who recite it for audiences

- Tragedy, like poetry, produces its effect without action - its power is in the mere reading; enacting it onstage should give the exact same effect as reading a good epic loud
- The tragedy is, in fact, superior, because it has all the epic elements as well as spectacle and music to provide an indulgent pleasure for the audience. Moreover, it maintains a vividness of impression in reading as well as staging.

Tragedy, then, despite the argument of critics is the higher art. And with this quite controversial conclusion Aristotle ends his work.

Analysis

Aristotle concludes the Poetics by addressing two main criticisms that often plagued poetry in his time. First, there is the question of what makes for 'good' poetry or 'bad' poetry. Aristotle points out that every work of art can be distilled to its 'essence,' meaning its purpose of imitation. Either a work aims to reveal life exactly as it is, as people think it is, or as it ought to be. Thus, depending on which of these three imitative purposes a poet has, his work should be considered under a separate set of criteria.

For instance, a poet who aims to show life as it 'ought to be' certainly has more relaxed standards for the accuracy of representation than a poet who is portraying life as it is. Aristotle uses the example of a poet who might not know that a hind does not have horns — in the case of a poet trying to portray life realistically, this error would ultimately be more glaring that in the case of a poet presenting an accurate view of life, simply because his purpose leads the reader to expect verisimilitude of detail.

That said, what is also significant for the reader to understand that in neither case does an error of detail necessarily affect the quality of the poem - unless it perverts the essence of the piece. Only if the author makes a fundamental error in the type of imitation he is pursuing is the final work ultimately compromised.

Aristotle ends by addressing what appears to be a long-standing debate between critics over the primacy of tragedy or epic poetry. Critics in his time vaunted epic poetry, but Aristotle takes the opposite view, noting that tragedy has all the same good qualities of an epic in its reading, but also has the added dimension of being able to translate onstage into a drama of spectacle and music, capable of being digested in one sitting.

Just as he began without much of an introduction, so too Aristotle finishes the Poetics with a perfunctory conclusion - no summary or final thought or discussion of significance. He wraps up his argument swiftly, content that he has addressed all the points laid out at the beginning, and confident that he has quashed his critics' preconceptions about the poetic art form.

Chapter 16

The Creative Instinct

In The Poetics, Aristotle asserts that literature is a function of human nature's instinct to imitate. This implies that as humans, we are constantly driven to imitate, to create. By labeling this creative impulse an "instinct," one is to believe that this desire for imitation is a matter of survival, of necessity. The question then arises, of what does one feel compelled to imitate and in what way does it aid in our survival? According to essays by T.S. Eliot and Barbara Johnson, the purpose of literature is to be a part of a necessary creative process, sometimes to the extent that the creator is lost and consumed by the cause.

The first issue to tackle is the question of what literature imitates. Imitation and representation encompass all the media of artistic expression with the artist striving to represent aspects of reality or human experience. This is done either through song, the visual arts, or literature. The artist, in a sense, strives to imitate God by wielding creative power and performing a human version of divine creation. The artist is attempting to communicate his or her subjective interpretation of the world. However, the use of an interpretive medium also poses a unique challenge. In the case of Literature, imitation is complicated by the inherent limitations of language.

Despite, or perhaps because of these limitations, artist then becomes part of a creative process in which the relationship between the writer, the text, and the subject matter become intertwined, blurring distinction between these separate components.

T.S. Eliot deals specifically with how one should view

literature in relation to its creator. He opposes the school of literary criticism that judges a poem's effectiveness based on the history and personality of the poet rather than the poem itself. According to Eliot, the poet must understand his or her position in the literary tradition. He states that "what is to be insisted upon is that the poet must develop or procure the consciousness of the past and that he should continue to develop this consciousness throughout his career". According to Eliot the only consciousness a writer should have is of his or her place in the literary tradition. Consciousness of emotional authenticity is irrelevant for Eliot. Consciousness of the literary past is what gives a text its individuality.

The individuality of the poet or the uniqueness of the emotions expressed in the poem is unnecessary because, Eliot believes, "one error, in fact, of eccentricity in poetry is to seek for new human emotions to express". Eliot wants the focus to be on the actual text for its contribution to the literary tradition rather than the poet's personality or emotional depth. Questions of whether or not the poem realistically captures human experience are not as important as whether the poem maintains its own emotional impact regardless of the poet's history. Therefore, if one understands imitation as the creator's representation of personal emotions or subjective experience, Eliot does not see imitation as the goal of literature. The poem is not representing something, but rather, it is existing on its own.

Despite the fact that Eliot does not see "mimesis" or, imitation as the goal of poetry, his theory of depersonalization of literature does relate to Aristotle's idea of mimesis. Eliot does not view the poet's personal experience as the proper motivation for good literature. During the creative process, the poet should experience "a continual surrender of himself as he is at the moment to something which is more valuable. The progress of an artist, is a continual self-sacrifice, a continual extinction of personality". However, this does not mean that the poet does not communicate emotional depth through poetry. A poet can still successfully capture certain epistemological and philosophical truths about existence and reality. He or she is still fulfilling the instinct to imitate. In fact, Elliot argues, only through depersonalization can the poet successfully communicate his imitation because it is not bogged down in subjective interpretation. Therefore, the poet is imitating and representing, but Eliot believes it is possible only by escaping the self and removing the personal implications of a text's meaning.

Barbara Johnson explores mimesis in relation to the limitations of language in her essay, "A Hound, a Bay Horse, and a Turtle Dove: Obscurity in Walden." Johnson focuses on Thoreau's use of symbolic language and what she sees as his unintended goal. She understands Thoreau's use of obscure symbols as representing an idea of obscurity rather than actual objects or concepts. She asserts that "You are supposed to recognize them as not as obscure symbols, but as symbols standing for the obscure, the lost, the irretrievable". In this sense, form follows content. The symbols are purposely obscure because they represent the irretrievable and obscure. Thoreau's imitation here is not relegated to a particular experience of loss, but of a concept and he accomplishes this in an intentionally cryptic fashion. This is because the concept he is attempting to communicate is itself so unknowable, so he uses obscure terms.

Thoreau realizes the limitations of language. He understood that the act of imitation is itself an endeavor limited by language. Therefore, for Thoreau, this instinctual impulse toward imitation remains exactly that - an impulse toward creativity despite the limitations of the medium. However, his text also maintains a consciousness of its inherent limitations. Johnson calls Thoreau's technique "catachreses," or, figurative substitutes for a literal term that does not exist. Thoreau fulfills his imitative instinct by using literature's representative, though inherently limited, faculty to represent something, which can not be represented.

Johnson concludes her essay by stating that Thoreau became so completely consumed in the creative act, that his figurative language ceases to be understandable as either pure rhetoric or a literal cataloguing of thoughts. She explains that, "what Thoreau has done in moving to Walden Pond is to move himself, literally, into the world of his own figurative language." His writing loses its coherence because his symbolism saturates and overwhelms the narrative. Johnson explains that "Thoreau has literally crossed over into the very parable he is writing, where reality itself has become a catachresis". He has delved so deeply into the act of representation that the reader is never sure of the creator's true intent. Perhaps it is Thoreau's intent to illustrate that the imitative power of literature is that one can never quite represent an idea, thought, emotions, without disclaiming its true intent beforehand. The paradox of artistic intent is that because of its inherent duality, art and literature can never specifically be separated from its creator or its product.

Both Eliot and Johnson agree that a text should posses a certain consciousness. For Eliot that consciousness is of the literary tradition, of the text of human experience. As Johnson demonstrates through Thoreau, text can not help but be conscious of its own limited imitative capacity. Eliot believes that if a poet depersonalizes a text enough, than it can really accomplish an expression of deep emotion or thought. Johnson sees the medium of literature as an obstacle to actual representation, but that ambiguity enhances the text to the extent that it "delights and baffles".

Aristotle's idea now takes on greater depth given these new perspectives. He phrases it as an "instinct towards imitation" because this impulse toward to creation is practically unconscious. As thoughtful beings, humans are driven to pursue this creative instinct. It is as innate an instinct for survival as the need for food and shelter. Therefore we pursue this impulse toward imitation almost without caring if we imitate successfully. We are acting within our given boundaries and limitations. According to Johnson, that is what gives literature its richness. Eliot believes the poet can transcend those limitations. Everyone agrees that one must act on the creative instinct.

Chapter 17

Paul Auster's Postmodernist Fiction: Deconstructing Aristotle's "Poetics"

Paul Auster is a storyteller. In an interview with Stephen Rodefer he stated: 'When I write, the story is always uppermost in my mind, and I feel that everything must be sacrificed to it.' He echoes Aristotle2 by recognising the logical priority of the story, although his postmodernist fiction denies any possibility of a teleological conception of art. Such art is ordered by a strict structure comprising of beginning, middle and end. The arrangement of the particular elements in its structure is governed by the universal principle to which everything must correspond. In Artistotle's "Poetics" fear and pity are the goal of tragedy, just as the ludicrous is the goal of comedy. I will also use this concept of teleological art in my essay in the context of classical art, defined by an idea that exists outside the text and which structures the logical ordering of its events. In particular, I will like to concentrate on the occasions when Auster's fiction seems to play with the predictability of such texts.

It is precisely with this promise of an 'easy' popular fiction that Auster lures the reader into reading his novels, spinning endless stories like a modern Scherhezade. Auster, however, uses conventions of popular fiction in order to foil them. With no principle of central organisation or authorial voice to give meaning to events, the narrative's logical sequence is disrupted. In the disjointed world of Paul Auster each fragment exists as a separate unit. With no causal order to link them together, the fragments are ruled by laws of random events and unpredictable chance.

Postmodernist fiction seems to reflect the fact that the writer has become tired of trying to explain a disjointed and godless universe. The classic narrative, according to Peter Brookes3, became a necessary means of organizing and interpreting the world as a consequence of the ideological failure of the 'sacred master plot.'

The task that Paul Auster tries to face is neither concerned with ordering nor explanation, it is rather a question of incorporating the chaos of the world 'beyond understanding' into his fiction. As Beckett indicated in an interview:

'What I am saying here does not mean that there will henceforth be no form in art. It only means that there will be a new form and that this form will be of such a type that it admits the chaos and does not try to say that the chaos is really something else[...] To find a new form that accommodates the mess, that is the task of the artist now.'

Umberto Eco in "Opera Aperta" calls open modern work 'an epistemological metaphor'; not only does it reflect aspects of modern philosophy and modern science but through its lack of conventional sense and order it represents the feeling of disorder and discontinuity that the modern world generates in all of us. Nothing could be better said of Paul Auster's fiction. The aim of this essay is to show how this 'ambiguity' of modern art is reflected upon.

The Story

Auster indicates in "The Art of Hunger" that the greatest influence on his work has been the fairy tales and oral tradition of storytelling. What he admires in these stories and tales is their economy of bare-boned narrative and lack of detail which leaves enough space in the text for the reader to inhabit it. The text acts as a 'springboard of imagination' and it is up to the reader to complete it. Similarly in "The New York Trilogy" Quinn says: 'in the good mystery there is nothing wasted, no sentence, no word that is not significant.' Under the central ordering of omnipotent narrator and promise of the 'salvation of a reader' due to the text's closure which will reveal it all, even the most insignificant detail cannot be overlooked.

As another version of teleological classic art, detective text is obsessed with closure; the end comes not only as a salvation of the reader but at the same time gives reassurance that the reader is not be wandering in a wilderness of ambiguous signs. Everything that happens in a detective story must be placed under the perspective of a final truth. The detective and the reader are deciphering the text under the watchful eye of the author who holds keys to the enigma. The detective pursues the truth using the power of reason and logic. Madeleine Sorapure8 states that the success of the detective is measured by the accuracy with which he emanates the 'transcendental reason of the author'.

Through establishing causality and eliminating ambiguity, the detective presents his own authorial ability to unite disparate elements into formal coherence. However, in "The City of Glass" the detective's pursuit of knowledge is frustrated. In an endless game of mirroring, Quinn demonstrates his inability to solve the mystery just as the narrator fails to decipher words from Quinn's red notebook, and inform us further of the hero's destiny:

'At this point the story grows obscure. The information has run out, and the events that follow this last sentence will never be known. It would be foolish even to hazard a guess.' As the detective proves unable to read the clues and the narrator fails to tell the story coherently, the interpretive desire of the reader becomes frustrated.

Russian formalism distinguishes between fabula and sjuzet, between the story to which the narrative refers and the plot which the author presents to us. In the case of "City of Glass", fabula would refer to the genre of popular detective fiction. Such fiction is reader oriented: its major characteristic being able to keep the reader or the listener in suspense for a long time and then surprise them by something he was far from expecting. Desire to find the body, evidence or the key to the enigma as desire to solve the crime becomes the telos of popular detective fiction. The sjuzet of the "City of Glass" deconstructs the intentions of the fabula and prevents this text from ever becoming popular detective fiction.

The form of the novel literally falls apart in progression as the reader is lead not towards the solution of the case but towards more confusion. William G. Little said that Auster's stories are not plot less but the plots are constantly foiled. In a story in which nothing happens, waiting for some sign or a message is equally futile; like waiting for Godot. In the meantime, the events have become increasingly obscure, characters drop off the pages without explanation, and meaning proliferates. It is not long before one realises that there will be no story at all.

The Aristotelian concept of plot is based upon definite structure and order: size and length are elements of beauty. The tragedy is an imitation of the action which is complete and whole. 'Component elements ought to be so firmly compacted that if any one of them is shifted to another place and removed, the whole is loosened up and dislocated'. Furthermore, Aristotle demands that the story does not start anywhere: well constructed stories would neither begin nor end at any chance point. The plot should be so structured that its elements are connected by logico-causal relation. If the whole telos of the tragedy is to produce feelings of fear and pity, then everything illogical, even if it did happen in reality, must be excluded from it, otherwise these feelings could not be induced. According to Aristotle the source of pleasure of the text comes from intellectual understanding. He opposes Plato by stating that the poet activates rational and not irrational thinking.

The poet's job is not to report what has happened but 'what is likely to happen'. The events should not be presented as they happen in life; rather they should follow the rules of necessity and probability. The best tragic imitation is of events which are fearful and pathetic, and these occurrences come best when they happen contrary to one's expectations yet logically, one following the other. It is in connection with these rules that Aristotle draws his aesthetic judgement of poetry as an endless creation that deals more with universal aspects of life which oppose history, the function of which is to reflect events as they occured. In life, however, things do not happen according to logic. Aristotle permits the irrational only in reality.

While the poet concentrates on imitation of only one action, the historian's duty is to describe the events as they happened. Samuel Farr is trying in the "In the Country of Last Things" to write a book which comprises endless stories of interviews of people about life in the city. Driven by the ambition to present a panoramic historical view of life in the city he collects all the stories without concentrating on a particular one. The result is that he ends up with a story so enormous that it is impossible for anyone to tell it, let alone read it.

However, Aristotelian logic and reasoning cannot be applied to the disjointed postmodern fiction of Auster. His story branches out in all directions, without a beginning, middle or end like some structureless 'rhizome'11... It reflects typically postmodern 'central emptiness under the absent god'. Absence of the ultimate divine truth, as absence of an organising centre or a frame, gives way to pagan proliferation of the meaning of the text. As a writer of fragments which exist alone 'with no before or after' he disrupts the linear progression of the story and relies on chance to move the plot forward. Thus, complexity opposes earlier linear ordering of cause and effect. Chance is an unpredictable and whimsical goddess, misused in 'bad' literature as a device that allows the writer freedom for endless possibilities and combinations. However, in Auster's fiction chance is a way of shattering the power of reason and logic as it occurs in his narrative.

The unexpected occurs with almost numbing regularity in our lives', he declares in "The Art of Hunger". As the improbable exists in reality, the task of the realist writer, as Paul Auster declares in " The Art of Hunger", is to use it as a source of imagination and present it in his fiction. Aristotle, on the other hand, advises the poet to choose events that are impossible but plausible 'in preference to ones that are possible but implausible'(Poetics,66p) because plots should not be made of irrational events. It seems to me that Auster's fiction is composed of these irrational events; this inexplicable and bewildering human existence challenges certainties and preconceptions of the world.

In "The Invention of Solitude" Auster remarks that his life is so fragmented that each time he sees a connection between two fragments, he is tempted to look for a meaning, to look beyond the facts of his existence.

Quinn comments in "City of Glass": 'nothing is real except the chance'. Auster's text centres around implications of chance. In an unpredictable universe, as Marco Fogg remarks in "Moon Palace", causality is no longer hidden demiurge that ruled the world, where down was up, first was last, the end was the beginning, the change is.the only constant. Steven Weisenburger suggests that through this philosophy of change, Marco Fogg glimpses the possibility of his own release from determinist metaphysics.

Baudrillard, in "Chance, Culture and the Literary Text" claimed that certain phenomena happen beyond our control and hence chance allowed certain space to escape responsibility for such phenomena. I do not argue that Auster had in mind the question of responsibility as much as his wish to express his bewilderment at the sense of contingency, which we are not aware of, present in our lives.

The challenge that Auster lays in front of the reader is to try to establish whether there is some pattern ruling the endless interplay of disparate events: a task similar to the endeavour of Quinn who stalks senior Stillman only to find out that the steps of the old man inscribe the letters 'Tower of Babel', suggesting fragmentation, chaos and confusion.

Quinn later wondered which words would spell his own steps in life. That is precisely what Auster does not wish us to know. He challenges our quest to determine by rationalising. There is no possibility of a solution or knowledge in Auster's fiction. Nashe in "The Music of Chance" is driven by the fact that certainly at some stage he will find out the truth; however he and the reader are denied the possibility of its discovery.

By stressing the impossibility of knowledge, Auster thus challenges what Lyotard14 calls one of the great legitimising myths of narrative archetypes: the speculative unity of knowledge. The breaking up of this snug unity of all knowing subjects is achieved through the presentation of something beyond our control, something that destroys the neat ordering of cause and effect: chance.

In an aftermath to their lost poker game, Nashe and Pozzi examine the reasons behind their failure. Pozzi as a poker player believes in chance and he is convinced that somewhere, sometimes he will be the chosen recipient of its good fortune. On a metaphysical level he expresses the belief in a world based upon a delicate harmony which must be maintained by care in order to keep its balance. He accuses Nashe of disturbing that balance and committing a sin by 'tempering with the universe'.

He broke the rhythm of their winning game by leaving the room at an inappropriate moment. The consequences for the destiny of the two heroes of "The Music of Chance" are catastrophic. Not only did they lose the game, but they were sentenced to hard labour. In order to pay for their gambling debt they had to build the wall.

The narrative moves away from freedom and movement, from the world played by music of chance into complete isolation and fixity of place. Nashe's attitude to his fate is fatalistic: he accepts the fact that his freedom is taken away from him as the building of the wall becomes some kind of atonement. He mocks Pozzi's belief in hidden purpose that explains how things work in the world be it luck, God or harmony. Once released from the world of chance with its indefinite possibilities of America's freeways he stoically tolerates his new position. It seems to me that "The Music of Chance" contrasts these two disparate worlds: improbable world of chance and determinate world of law. In the world of chance Nashe's existence comes as 'the fixed point in a whirl of changes'. In the world of restriction and order, the body is under strict surveillance and must adhere to the law. The challenge that Pozzi and Nashe must overcome is the building of the wall. This wall, which becomes a postmodern pastiche of its origins as an Irish castle to produce something new, is a way of separation of these two worlds. The closer they get to finishing, the further away they are from their freedom until eventually it becomes a wall of terror they are building around their lives.

As if the determinate world of law and order needs the wall in order to protect itself from the improbabilities of freedom and chance. The wall is menacing; it bears the restriction with it, just as the Sea Wall project from "In the Country of Last Things", it is designed also to keep the disenchanted subjects from escaping.

'Reality is a Chinese box, an infinite series of containers within containers', says Paul Auster in an interview in "Art of Hunger". It seems that every time he manages to find certain links between disparate elements he feels the urge to celebrate: Auster's fiction is full of little anecdotes that show the unpredictability of life. In these inexplicable events which point out that life is not as straightforward as one hoped it would be, Auster finds the roots of his imagination: reality is stranger than fiction. In "The Invention of Solitude" Auster presents the story called "The first commentary on the nature of chance":

'This is where it begins. During the war M.'s father had hidden out from Nazis for several months in a Paris chambre de bonne. Eventually, he managed to escape, made his way to America, and began a new life. Years passed more than twenty years M. had been born, had grown up, and was now going off to study in Paris. Once there, he spent several difficult weeks looking for a place to live. Just when he was about to give up in despair, he found a small chambre de bonne. Immediately, upon moving in he wrote a letter to his father to tell him the good news. A week or so later he received a reply: your address, wrote M.'s father, that is the same building I hid out during the war.'

This is the root of Paul Auster's writing. The game of writing that starts 'when nothing can be explained anymore', because the bewildering experience reduces one to silence. This silence precedes the writing. The imagination that springs out from the presence of extraordinary reality is what haunts him and propels him to reach deep into the depths of his memory in order to find a whole world within the walls of inner self. Memory is, for Auster, an inner myth comprising of endless life stories which come to mind involuntarily, because we cannot order what to remember. Presented as childhood stories and anecdotes of his life. In Auster's fiction, memory also becomes a restructuring of the historical past: as an immersion in the life of others. The memory of being a Jew, memory of the Holocaust as memory of the unspeakable, haunts Auster. Furthermore, memory is described as a space in which the event happens for the second time.

Memory is also referred to as a body, as a skull, as a room, as a place, as a building. Auster shares Saint Augustine's thoughts on memory 'as a vast immeasurable sanctuary, buried deep inside one's soul, which retains primacy in the understanding of one's mind.' Memory comes, according to Auster, as a voice to one's inner mind which is not necessarily one's own; 'this voice that speaks to him in a way a voice might tell stories to a child, yet at times this voice makes fun of him'. It is the voice also of the 'possessed' that associates Auster with the prophets: Jeremiah, who couldn't speak in the presence of the Lord so God put forth his hand and put his words into his mouth.

Memory of the 'I' who has vanished from itself and cannot be heard except as another. What myth is for Aristotle's plot, memory is for Auster's story. This myth moulded in solitude is based not on tradition, as Aristotle would have liked, but upon ruthless examination of self. What brings Auster to Thoreau and Hawthorne is a belief that literature is forged in isolation and working on oneself. Memory is, therefore, mythology of the inner soul, which comprises all the stories our consciousness weaves inside of us. However, memory as we have seen from "In the Country of Last Things" also forms the basis of language. Memory happens in spite of oneself, we cannot choose what to remember and what to forget: thus in the city where objects are constantly disappearing their names are being forgotten too. The trouble is that not everyone forgets the same thing: when Anna asks the guard about the aeroplane he doesn't know what it is. He even accuses her of making up stories. She can get in trouble for making up stories because the government does not like it. With no common ground to go on people of the city could become locked inside their own solipsistic language.

Paul Auster is not the storyteller that Walter Benjamin had in mind when describing the art of storytelling.The inspiration of the story comes from a pool of oral tradition and experience passed by the word of mouth. There the storyteller has counsel for the listener, his counsel is wisdom. Memory plays a vital part in the transmission of a storyteller's message: it must be remembered in order to be retold. This is reminiscent of the narration of Cashinahua Indians that Lyotard mentions in "Just Gaming", which is just another example of how the collective whole can have a role in the transmission of the message.

The case of Paul Auster, it appears to me, is of another sort: the source of storytelling comes from isolation, from the solitude of an artist who sits alone in a room and writes with no particular purpose in mind except a compelling urge to write, the writer who sought refuge in order to create. The story of Auster's inner experience collected as memory does provoke listening.

Although his experiences shape the story, Auster autobiographic details are given only as a detail of the character's life, amongst other voices that speak in the text. Auster often expresses a desire to implicate his authorial self in his text. Even when he speaks about himself as we can see from Auster's text, the author does not speak with a direct language of his own, rather he introduces himself amongst a multitude of other perspectives in a polyphony of discourse. 'The self whose name appears on the covers of books is finally not the same self that writes the book', says Auster in "The Art of Hunger". Fictional details of Auster's life cannot be so easily equated with his real life.

The writing itself imposes such distance, so I would agree with Blanchot, that this distance\neutralises beforehand all meaning or lack of it. This is the distance of the artist who in order to create, has disintegrated his own self, until his story becomes incomprehensible, until 'it speaks in neuter'.

The theme of the absent father is recurrent in Auster's story. His first prose fiction "The Invention of Solitude", written after his father's death, was an attempt to fill in the void left by his absence. Auster is painfully aware of the absurdity of his task, of the impossibility of entering another's solitude: the man would let you get as far as he wants you to come. Auster's father is the epitome of the postmodern character: 'an impenetrable space in the block of time'. The figure of the father looms in the background of Auster's fiction. In the "City of Glass" the father-son relationship is translated into an oppressive tale of innocent sons and their vicious fathers.

Stillman senior performs a language experiment on his offspring: he wants to implement God's language by denying his son the human language. He keeps him in the dark room for many years, he crushes him into submission. It is the word of the father that the child must obey. Just like in Kafka's story "The Judgement" where Herr Bendemann pronounces death by drowning, a sentence his son readily obeys. However, the father's language experiment in "City of Glass" does not work; it creates a puppet without identity. Submission to authority causes the self to lose its voice: 'Perhaps I am Peter Stillman. Perhaps I am not. My real name is Peter Nobody.' In this light, the theme of disaffiliation as Chris Tysh describes it, becomes a way of escaping from closure of divine truth or authority of oppressive fathers.

"City of Glass" deconstructs the father's divine language and records the Babel like confusion and decay. However, "Moon Palace" offers another version of tale of origin. Narrated in concentrated circles, it evolves around the three generations of complete strangers who belong to the same family. Chance encounters bring unforeseen changes to their lives: at the centre of this disfunctional family universe is the comical overweight figure of Julian Barber who, as the story turns out, is Marco's father. For Aristotle these moments of 'recognition' between members of close family bear not only intense drama but bring about 'peripety' of the dramatic action. For Auster it is just another story which boils down to a series of missed chances.

The pieces of jigsaw puzzle are there from the beginning but nobody bothers to fit them together. All the movements in the novel are cyclical; no sooner does Marco Fogg finish one cycle of his life than he begins another, until he ends up literally at the end of the world beyond which there is nothing except emptiness. As the Moon finds its way in the darkness of the sky, Marco ponders about the new beginning. The Moon has a feminine, repetitive nature. It is the object of desire, the urge to capture it is seen as a symbol of progress. It also, as Byrne said in the novel, helps define man's position on Earth. As Marco wanders around New York like forsaken Adam whose life becomes total chaos and decay, he overhears the words of the American president who greets the first steps on the Moon as the greatest in the history of humanity.

The theme of hunger is another important feature of Auster's story. Image of a hungry artist links him to Knut Hamsun and Kafka. It expresses the hunger of the artist for whom the writing has become a compulsion and matter of survival. It expresses Auster's idea of writing as compulsion and the obsession of the artist who must write in order to stay alive. The art becomes need, necessity and desire. Auster's essays on literature are published under the title "The Art of Hunger". The artist who produces the art of hunger starves to create. In order that Sam Farr may continue writing his story about the city, he must do without: all the money that he has is spent on paying people to come and talk to him. He is aware that if he stops writing he would be lost, because the book is the only thing that keeps him going.

To live in the city he must write, to carry on writing, he must starve. Another important connection between speaking and writing is mentioned in Auster's essay about Louis Wolfson. Adam was granted the privilege of naming the creatures of Paradise and was later expelled for having eaten from the tree of knowledge. Mystics fast in order to receive the word of God. The body of Christ, the word made flesh, says Auster, is eaten in holy communion. Similarly, food is the favourite subject of conversation in "In the Country of Last Things". The stories about food are told according to a strict protocol. One must never laugh and never allow the hunger to take over. Anna Blumme calls these stories the "ghost stories".

Marco Fogg's anorexia on the other hand comes as a form of resistance. This protest against society is refined to the form of aesthetic nihilism, through radical refusal to do anything to help his position. He is certain that once the money runs out he is going to starve and possibly die but still he resolves to do nothing as a form of protest to the world. He decides to become living proof that something is rotten in the land of plenty. Similarly in a short story by Kafka,22 the aesthetics of hunger receives most meticulous elaboration. The story is called "The Fasting Showman" and is centred upon the figure of a hunger artist who is sitting in a cage performing his art of fasting. His eagerness to show off his skill prompts him to stretch out his arms through the bars so people might feel how thin they are.

He takes painstaking measures to make sure that his art of fasting is genuine, although he is watched day and night by the guards he even whistles in their presence to let them know that he is not helping himself to some nourishment in secret. He fasts in order to be admired, however the public gradually loses its taste for his art and he dies in the straw of his forgotten cage. The theme of hunger and starvation can also be applied to the body of the modern text. Mark Anderson in his text "Anorexia and Modernism, or How I learned to diet in all directions" maintains that the text is moving towards the starvation caused by 'hermeneutic blockage common to twentieth century minimalism'. This aesthetic approach to the text comes as a modernist response to the fragmentation, ephemerality and contingency which characterise modern life. It also, I think, reflects the rejection of the conventional language of classic novels. Paul Auster in "The Art of Hunger" criticises the writer who does too much 'overwhelming the reader with so many details that he no longer has any air to breathe. 'A character comes to the room. How much of that room do you want to talk about?', asks Paul Auster (The Art of Hunger, p205). In order to make it new the postmodernist writers must spit out the old language of classic narratives as fattening. As 'the body of the language' shrinks causing the story to disintegrate and confuse us, it is now up to the reader to join the loose threads of the story together and give them meaning. The text thus moves away from the author to the reader. Aristotle counts upon the reader to accomplish tragic catharsis while Auster relies upon him to risk his sanity and work out what is happening in his text. However, the discipline of self-starvation governing the thin body of Auster's postmodernist fiction leads to interpretative collapse on the part of the reader. No matter how hard he tries, the emaciated story always escapes him, until the reader is left with the feeling that nothing is sure and nothing adds up.

The Character

Aristotle in "Poetics" gives the plot such prominence that he states that tragedy cannot exist without a plot, but it can without characters. Plot is an imitation of action and is enacted by the people performing that action. Plot is not based upon the unity of a single person. Homer in the"Odyssey" did not incorporate everything that happened to his hero, because he would have to include an indefinite amount of events that can happen to a given individual. Demands of the poetic mimesis required that he compose his story around a single unified action. The structure of the plot, states Aristotle, is the goal of the tragedy and the goal is of the greatest imortance. Aristotle's concept of character in "Poetics" is ethical: character is defined by making ı moral choice, the decision borne out of careful consideration. In "Poetics" the character is defined by 'that kind of utterance which clearly reveals the bent of man's moral choice', hence Aristotle concludes that there is no character in that class of utterance where there is nothing at all that the speaker is selecting or rejecting.

If we apply Aristotle's theory to the postmodern fiction of Paul Auster, the conclusion would be that there is no character in his novel. In Auster's fiction, where language is unstable and nothing is real except chance, his characters are not the central point around which the text revolves. Who Quinn is and where he comes from, and what he has done are of no great importance, says Auster. Aristotle on the other hand gives much thought in his text to the concept of character. Tragedy is the imitation of people 'who are to be taken seriously'.

The audience needs to identify with their actions and feel sympathy towards them in order to feel tragic catharsis when their fate is transformed from good fortune into bad. Also, virtuous man should not experience a change in fortunes from good to bad nor should wicked man experience a change from bad fortune to good. The ideal hero should fall between these extremes: he is neither a paragon of virtue nor the epitome of evil. Change of his destiny from happiness to misfortune did not happen because of some wickedness, but because of some mistake. Aristotle correctly anticipates that the spectator's perception of fear depends upon the judgement that the sufferer did not deserve his misfortune, therefore, it could happen to anyone. The characters should be good; their action should reveal a sound moral judgement.

Furthermore, they should be appropriate and consistent, the characteristic that was later adopted as a poetic rule of decorum. The appropriate character shows traits that correspond to his class and sex: if the poet represents the woman 'she should not be made to be brave or clever'. The characters also act with consistency They should be realistic in a way that they should show a 'likeness to human nature.' The feeling of pity will be aroused when the spectator feels for someone who is similar to him, because he is actually afraid that the same thing could happen to himself. If the character is known from Greek tradition, his actions must resemble an already established prototype. The rules of probability and necessity govern the consistency of character: his actions at all times should follow logic.

If the idea of character implies the centre as a governing logic that follows either a realistic, psychological or other logic that follows either a realistic, psychological or other causal explanation, then it is clear that Auster's fiction is characterless. Hans Berten in "Exploring Postmodernism" maintains that postmodernist characterisation presents the character as unknowable.

Auster challenges the concept of character as defined by an untouched identity buried deep inside oneself. He also rejects the notion of the consistent journey with evolving and developing personality that is mastered through hard work of self-discovery.

In a world of fragments where language reflects the split between words and their objects, the character is de-centred in an endless play of signification. A dislocated subject cannot find stability in a world ruled by random forces and unstable language. On his way back from visiting Peter Stillman, Quinn sees a tree and wonders whether this tree has the same significance for Peter as for himself. If this tree is not the same for Peter, Quinn asks himself what it really was. The words and their representations are out of control and that affects the characters' ability to establish themselves. Auster's characters tend to move away from origin and authority, towards a dionysiac forgeting of the self. Certain conclusions about their actions cannot be drawn: they have no centre nor stable identity.

The only consolation left to Auster's subject is to reinvent himself: uncle Victor says in "Moon Palace" that every person is the author of his own life. Auster's characters very easily assume someone else's identity. Quinn becomes Paul Auster, the detective called upon to solve the mystery. To become someone else is a form of consolation for Quinn. It offers the lightness of becoming the other, of being on the surface with no inner thoughts, while the burden of your own consciousness gets forgotten. He also uses the pseudonym of William Wilson to write detective novels.

Athough within he was born as Daniel Quinn, he gave birth to many other personalities; thus Wilson becomes the creature that lives an independent existence to that of the mainstream consciousness of his inner self. Quinn treats

Wilson sometimes with admiration, sometimes with deference. He is aware that Wilson leads an independent life, the truth is that Quinn has stopped thinking of himself as real, if he had lived at all, he lived through the imaginary life of Max Work, the detective hero of his novels. The more Work continued to live in the outside world, the more removed from the world Quinn became. He seemed to have vanished within the space of his own hermetic existence.

The process here becomes reversed: Work becomes real while Quinn becomes fiction. Sam Farr in "In The Country of Last Things" assumes the identity of a doctor at Woburn House. Here, as Dr Farr his situation mirrors his life inside the Library, he listens to people's stories once again. Through his new persona of benevolence he gains access to the intimate thoughts of others. As he is in the position of a person who wears the white coat and sympathetic look on his face, he finds the way to listen to people's stories without being crushed by them: 'it is better not having to be myself', he remarks.

The question of identity is what turns Paul Auster's character into a subject whose main ontological purpose becomes 'working out questions', in a bid to establish its own being in an unreliable world. 'The question of who is who and whether or not we are who we think we are' is what interests Auster. The subject is involved in a confirmation of his own rational processes, however the author grants no possibility of knowledge.

Quinn's eagerness to solve his case leads nowhere, in a process of looking for clues he loses all the leads. His investigation turns out to be the investigation of the reality itself, as his case becomes obscure and witnesses disappear without a trace. His continuing obsessive dedication to it takes him to the end of himself: he is finally broken in pieces like some fallen figure of Humpty-Dumpty. Thus Humpty-Dumpty becomes not only the symbol of the subject's fall; but also of the fragmentation that has taken place. This fragmentation is manifested in "Moon Palace" as a literal disintegration of the body:

'Then I imagined my head cracking open, splattering like

the eggs that had fallen to the floor of my room. I felt my brains dribbling out of me. I saw myself in peices.'

The theme of the dissintegration of Auster's subject comes as a consequence to a loss of identity and is manifested in physical terms as a shattering of the body. Fogg in "Moon Palace" wears his uncle's suit all year around at the college. He imagined that the suit was holding him together and if he did not wear it his body would fall apart. Isabel "In the Country of Last Things" dies of an genetic disease which causes disintegration of the body. The lack of centre causes Auster's subjects to lead restless existences. It causes them to lose touch with themselves and turn into perpetual outsiders of their own lives.

Marco Fogg felt that he was flying in greater and greater circles around himself until he span out of orbit. This breaking up of the identity is manifested visually in the portrait of Auster's father taken in Atlantic city studio: given as the image of his father shot from different angles so that the viewer is under the impression that several men are sitting around the table staring vacantly into the space. Auster calls this image the portrait of an invisible man. It also reflects the impossibility of saying anything without reservation: 'he was good or he was bad, he was this or he was that. All of them are true. At times I have the feeling that I am writing about three or four different men, each one distinct, each one a contradiction of all the others.' The theme of disintegration is applied to the author of the text as well.

In order to write, observes Auster in "The Art of Hunger", he has to treat himself as if he was someone else. The writing thus, as Barthes would say (S/Z), becomes the destruction of every point of origin. Disintegration on a metaphysical level brings about the shattering of the unitary consciousness of the author as originator and ruler of the truth. Auster's text speaks in multitude of voices without any one being singled out as the author's unique discourse.

In the uncertain disjointed world of Paul Auster's fiction, the subject can only experience its own existence through another. Watching, stalking the other, as Blue does in "Ghosts", brings one only closer to oneself. The outside world has become the window through which he stalks Black, describing his every move. He is aware of the complexity of his job: the surveillance has to be constant for the whole picture may change with a moment of inattention. However, seeing is not believing, Blue cannot find solace in the unity of truth which comprises of 'I perceive'.

However hard he tries to find out about Black by watching him, he does not get any closer to the truth. Blue slowly finds himself thinking about things that have never occurred to him before: by watching the other he starts to watch himself. Not that he had ever before given thought to what happens inside of him; the world within was a dark, unexplored territory. Blue feels like a man condemned to sit in a room and go on reading a book for the rest of his life. He could little by little get so caught up in the story and begin to forget himself. But the book offers him nothing.

The question that Blue is trying to work out, while his whole life is on hold, is how to get out of the situation brought on by his compulsion to carry on watching Black. The situation of Blue is similar to that of the writer; it requires the same solitude and the same desire. However, perception will not bring the object closer; it will not lead to the knowledge of how things work in the world. The more Blue watches Black, the more he learns about his habits, the more he is convinced that he really does not know the man. Blue has to write a report on Black. He is even contemplating to include in the report various stories he has made up himself but decides not to do so, this is not the story of his life.

Instead, he resolves to stay in line with the truth: reducing himself to describe events as he saw them. Soon he becomes aware of the absurdity of his task: words do not necessarily correspond to reality, they rather obscure what they are meant to say. This is what Stillman senior tries to accomplish by creating langue pure: to restore a disjointed world into a former unity by mending the gap between the words and their representations. In order to accomplish his task he sifts through the rubbish of New York, cataloguing the broken objects, giving them their new names, like some parody of Adam in the garden of Eden. Blue watches Black until he can no longer trust what he sees, wondering if is possible that such a man, who merely sits in his room and writes, actually exists. Perception does not bring the other closer to knowledge or truth. Uncertainty is at the core of Auster subject causing the confusion about their own self.

As the outer thus usurps the sovereignty of the inner, Auster's subject feels most comfortable in closed spaces. For only in solitude we can know who we are because we can think of who we are. Auster displays a fundamentally solipsistic view of man. Man is an island, his true presence happens only in loneliness.

Solitude, says Auster is a terryfying prospect of the 'I' who has vanished from itself and can speak only through the voice of another. The connection between self and other which was not possible to achieve by perception, can be achieved in solitude. Through learning about oneself the man is able to connect to other.

That is the reason why Auster does not think that solitude is a gloomy idea. 'It is simply fact, one of the conditions of being human and even if we're surrounded by others we essentially live our lives alone: real life takes place inside of us.' The solitude represents, on one hand, the solitude of the writer who sits alone in his room and writes for days and days. Auster remarks in "Red Notebook" our sense of self is formed by the pulse of consciousness within us; as an endless monologue, the story that our inner self weaves inside us.

Solitude comes with the comfort of closed spaces; the room at 6 Varvick Streeet from "The Book of Memory", where a man has retired from the world in order to write. The time of the season is the winter, a 'hermetic season, a long moment of inwardness'.

This room has become man's second skin. The room is filled in with his inner thoughts, its walls becoming the pillars of his own consciousness. It is only within this Aristotelian unity of time and space that the subject feels most comfortable. The comfort Quinn experiences when his world shrinks to the size of the room in Stillman's apartment. The only thing he knows for certain is that the interminable exchange of darkness and light will go on forever, as he observes it through the window. He thinks of his life before the story began. He says goodbye to William Wilson and Max Work. He is finally able to write his observations in the red notebook under his real name. He writes about the stars, the earth and hopes for mankind.

He feels that his words are now part of the world at large 'as real and specific as a stone, or a lake or a flower'. Solitude does not only come as a form of the person who refuses having to face what lies within himself or having to be seen by anyone else. Such is the picture of Auster's father given as the portrait of an invisible man unknown to himself or others, the man lost without a centre who was a 'tourist of his own life'.

Auster's subjects experience a desire to crawl back into the womb in order to give second birth to the subject 'within the mental uterus of a closed space'.26 Solitude is symbolised in a recurrent image of Jonah praying for deliverance while trapped in a belly of the whale.

The solitude of Nashe, who 'crazy with loneliness' tries to work out questions for himself, believing that certainly the truth will reveal itself to him. The solitude of Marco Fogg who in despair decided to spit on the world and starve as a form of protest. The loneliness of Quinn who moves through morass of objects trying to find an idea that holds them together. The solitude of the postmodern man who is refused the 'solace of an identity' in an uncertain world.

The only consolation for Auster's subject is to be within a closed space of a room, because only in a room he can be himself, can wonder within himself to find a whole world there. The space in Auster's fiction is inseparable from its subject. However, only in a closed space can Paul Auster's subject feel comfortable for there he can exerience his identity as a cartesian unity of the one who thinks and therefore is.

'The world has shrunk to the size of this room for him, and for as long as it takes him to understand it, he must stay where he is. Only one thing is certain: he cannot be anywhere until he is here. And if he does not manage to find this place it would be absurd for him to look for another.'

The closed room is the metaphor for writing. In this most intimate and hidden place the writer weaves his stories. (Like Fanshawe who gives his last manuscript behind the closed doors). When Marco Fogg in "Moon Palace" is forced to leave his room and abandon it, he adopts the cave in Central Park. Closed space is the only protection for a subject in pieces. It also acts as a shield that prevents the outside from coming to further usurp the sanctity of the inside. The space in the form of the outside becomes the city, where in order to stay alive subject must learn how to read the signs. City is an ideal space for the poet. Auster says in "The Art of Hunger":

'if the poet's primary obligation is to see, there is a similar though less obvious injuction upon the poet; the duty of not being seen. In order to see, the poet must make himself invisible. He must disappear, eface himself in anonymity.

Auster further maintains that only in the modern city can the one who wants to remain unseen find his place. However, even as he becomes part of landscape, the poet is always the outsider. The city is also a space where Auster's subjects embark upon the journey of discovery in the vain hope of rationalising it and giving meaning to their own existence. The city is menacing in "In the Country of Last Things" and commits its citizens to absolute loyalty, it requires abolition of the self in order to survive. Anna Blumme's knowledge in a city remains always inadequate; it seems that nobody has an overall picture of the life in it.

While the questions of her brother's disappearance that she came to solve remain unsolved, the terror of living in the city come from the fact that nothing is clear and no one knows for sure. Space "In the Country of Last Things" becomes a cite of where body is put under restriction: its subjects cannot leave or have any burial, their dead bodies are used for fuel, for keeping the city going.

The concept of space as a construction of a certain social order becomes clear as the city's attempt to control the starved bodies of its inhabitants.

The Meaning

When it comes to meaning, Paul Auster has no poetic programme: 'the question is the story itself and what does it mean is not for the story to tell', he declares in "City of Glass". However, in "The Invention of Solitude" he also states that the function of the story is to make a man see something before his eyes by holding up another thing to view and in so doing delight him into a new feeling of life.

The act of writing thus becomes the process of discovery, a battle, as Auster says, to rescue each moment from a confusion through the purity of perception. As I mentioned earlier, in order to achieve the goal of seeing, the poet must disappear and efface himself in anonymity.

He must become the solitary wanderer, a faceless scribe as his poetry becomes 'an act of loneliness.' (The Art of Hunger,) In order to delight the reader into a new feeling of life, the poet watches the world as an outsider would. For Paul Auster to be an outsider is to be Jewish, thus he often mentions the words of Marina Tsvetaeva: 'In this most Christian of worlds/all poets are Jews.' A similar idea is expressed by Edmond Jabe when interviewed by Paul Auster:

'The condition of being a writer has little by little become almost the same as being a Jew. I feel that every writer in some way experiences the Jewish condition, because every writer, every creator lives in a kind of exile.'

The more the poet watches the outside, the more he becomes aware that the world does not correspond to a a definite pattern of knowlege. The meaning has become whatever one wishes to become, the result of endless play of signification.

The relation between signifier and signified is not defined as a unity that is outside the text, it is rather manifested as the arbitrary relation between the word and its concept. Stillman wants to mend this division between signifier and signified and his mission is to restore the primordial unity of words and their representations as perceived as a desire to restore the human spirit.

Aristotle's concept of poetic text implies that the poet constructs the plot using the well known material from Greek mythology. The poet's innovation, therefore, is severely constricted: his originality is expressed by the way in which events in the plot are created, which elements of the story are presented, and which are left to the imagination of the audience. The poet cannot significantly change the traditional story. Aristotle also advises poets 'not to cling at all costs to the traditional plots around which [...] tragedies are constructed'. The poet can, therefore, invent the plot as long as he follows the laws of probability and necessity.

The structure of the story must be organised so it can produce the effect of fear and pity. In order to achieve these feelings the reader must empathise with the author's intention. The text becomes the place where the unity of the author's intentions and reader 's expectations is achieved; the reader must acquire the author's intended meaning. Without tragic catharsis, Aristotle believes there is no tragedy. Classic text, I think, implies a certain contract between the author who is a producer of the text and the reader who is a consumer of it. This contract binds the writer to follow the logic of predictability when ordering events. The freedom of the reader as a recipient of the text is limited to the interpretation of the text as the author intended.

The meaning is defined as the message that the author sends to the reader. Aristotle's aesthetics are based upon the idea that text cannot produce just any kind of pleasure. His aesthetic judgment of the tragedy is based upon the effectiveness of the construction of the plot in order to achieve feelings of fear and pity.

On the other hand the aesthetic of the postmodern text is based upon the gap between presentation and reality. Auster is increasingly becoming aware that in writing there exists a gap between thinking and writing, that the story the writer is about to tell us somehow escapes language:

'Never before have I been so aware of the rift between thinking and writing. For the past few days, in fact, I have begun to feel that the story I am trying to tell is somehow incompatible with language, that the degree to which it resists language is an exact measure of how closely I have come to saying something important and then when the moment arrives for me to say one truly important thing, I will not be able to say it.'

This aesthetic of the sublime, 'the unrepresentable' is based upon Kant's idea of the difference between our faculty to present something and conceive of it. In Auster's text the sublime is based upon the reality which strikes Auster as stranger than we think, and he wishes to incorporate these instances of inconceivable events into his text. Thus as I have attempted to argue he brakes the linear ordering of events by introducing chance, by denying his subject the knowledge of truth and by dispersing the notion of a unity of consciousness of the author lying behind the text.

Like Auster, Aristotle maintains that events in reality may not be connected by logic. He thus permits the irrational only in reality but not in the poetic text. Poetry is, therefore, more universal than history. History imitates the particular events as they randomly happen, while poetry presents events connected by logic of probability and necessity. Aristotle passes aesthetic judgement on poetry, claiming that it shares its universality with philosophy and is therefore more valuable than history.

The postmodern fiction of Paul Auster is based upon the idea that there is no unique meaning of the text. While the logic of metanarrative orders the Aristotle's conception of text30 (as with organising of narrative events according to an idea which is outside of the text), Auster's postmodern text does not represent, I think, a space where the interraction between reader and author is taking place.

In a constant shifting of meaning, the words do not point to something outside the language, rather meaning is achieved through their endless interraction and combination. Meaning has become the activity of reading,31 a matter of interpretation, as the text shifts away from the author: 'I finally believe it's the reader who writes the book and not the writer' says Auster in " The Art of Hunger".

Similarly, Barthes in S/Z says that the meaning of the text is established in a process of reading. The meaning is established through 'deja lu' codes, of 'already read.' It's 'already read' (used here as predictable narrative of lisible text) that Auster's story often implies when it tries to goad the reader into accepting it as just another traditional text. Auster's text relies on 'already read' which is being deconstructed as the text moves away from a traditional, classical narrative. (As explained earlier in the text as a difference between fabula and sjuzet).

As a postmodern text, Auster's text avoids the end, closure. He rejects the notion that the text's narrative is dominated by knowledge of end: the end which can finally determine the meaning, closing sentence as signifying totality:

'The closer you come to the end, the more there is to say. The end is only imaginary, a destination you invent to keep yourself going, but a point comes when you realise you will never get there. You might have to stop, but that is only because you have ran out of time. You stop but that does not mean you have come to the end.' (In the Country of Last Things,)

In a disjointed fiction of Paul Auster the reader becomes similar to "the object hunter" from "In the Country of Last Things". As an object hunter you must make your living by collecting discarded objects, rescuing things before they reach the state of absolute decay. You can never count on finding anything intact, because that's the mistake on a part of a person who lost it. In the novel of 'disappearing story' (as postmodern fiction moves away from the idea of story as a linear ordering of events), such as Auster's, the reader becomes the object-hunter who tries to connect the intact islands which make sense and join them together into a new continent of meaning. He painstakingly attempts to make sense of the story. No matter how hard he tries the meaning always escapes him.

The plurality of meaning of the postmodern text is achieved by breaking up of the "sacred" entity between the writer and the reader. The text is taken from the author and thrown like a bottle into the sea. This image Lyotard paints in

"Just Gaming" to express the idea that the writers write 'without knowing for whom they are speaking'.

The reading, one could agree with Barthes, of a classical text has become a stereotypical act: the predictability of the such a text means that the reader is assured that eventually the author's message will be revealed to him.

The message of the postmodern text thrown like the bottle in the sea, associtess me of the short story by Kafka called the "A Message From the Emperor":

'The Emperor -so the story goes-has sent a message to you, the lone individual, the meanest of all the subjects, the shadow that has fled before the imperial sun until it is microscopic in the remotest distance, just to you the Emperor has sent a message from his death-bed.'

However, the messenger never gets to the end of the chambers of the innermost palace, even if he eventually struggles to leave the innermost gate, he would still have the capital city to leave and then 'centre of the world, overflowing with dregs of humanity.'(A Message from the Emperor, p136). The message was never meant to be delivered.

The meaning of the postmodern text reflects the plurality of the Babel-like inspired fragmentation of language. The poet's word, as Paul Auster describes in "The Art of Hunger", reminds him of Cassandra's word. A beautiful daughter of Priam, endowed with prophetic powers by Apollo. Punished later for her infidelity with the curse that her prophetic words are never to be believed. For Auster it symbolises the words of the poet, spoken again and again in order to say nothing.

Chapter 18

Aristotle's Poetics

Complexity and Pleasure: Aristotle's 'Complex Plot' and the pleasure element in tragedy

First, the instinct of imitation is implanted in man from childhood, one difference between him and other animals being that he is the most imitative of living creatures, and through imitation learns his earliest lessons; and no less universal is the pleasure felt in things imitated. We have evidence of this in the facts of experience. Objects which in themselves we view with pain, we delight to contemplate when reproduced with minute fidelity.

In his *Poetics* Aristotle (384-322 BC) classifies plot into two types: simple [haplos], and complex [peplegmenos]. The simple plot is defined as a unified construct of necessary and probable actions accompanied by a change of fortune. The complex plot, says Aristotle, is accompanied by two other features, namely; peripeteia or reversal, and anagnorisis, or recognition.

It is this which Aristotle feels is the best kind of tragic plot, in that it provides the best possibility of delivering tragic pleasure. Before we look at the distinctive features of the complex plot, it would perhaps be instructive to examine those features which it shares with the simple plot. The unity of structure recommended by Aristotle includes the tripartite division of the plot into the beginning, the middle and the end, as well as the unities of time and action. He stresses unified action, where all action in the plot carries a definite link to other actions, and subsequent actions are the necessary and probable outcomes of the former.

Necessary and probable are terms which recur throughout the *Poetics*. They stand for the universality of poetry in that they point to how or what actions should logically be in a given situation. Unity of action, therefore, does not mean all that happens to the protagonist, but precisely what comprises a particular whole action according to the norms of necessity and probability. Unity of time, in contrast to its neo-classical applications, here simply means the time span in which the tragic action can be best comprehended by the audience, given the constraints of human memory, and the wholeness of the action.

Finally, we come to the change of fortune. It is either from good to bad or the reverse. The former is more characteristic of tragedy but in a later section Aristotle complicates the idea by saying that those plots where the catastrophe is averted by recognition are best. The change of fortune is also accompanied by a complication of events [desis] and their resolution [lusis].

Having briefly examined the common aspects of both kinds of plot, we can now look at the special attributes of the complex plot.

Let us take another look at Aristotle's celebrated definition of complex action: 'A complex action is one where the change is accompanied by such reversal or recognition or both.' Peripeteia has been defined as a reversal of the action. If, however, it is just that, then how is it different from the change of fortune? Clearly this is too limited a definition of peripeteia and it would perhaps be pertinent to consider two other definitions. Humphrey House defines it as a 'reversal of intention'. This definition takes into account the 'thought' or the dianoia exercised by the character. House describes it as 'holding the wrong end of the stick'. Peripeteia is therefore the turning of the stick thinking that it is the right end. The ignorance behind any peripeteia is not mere ignorance. It is the ignorance arising out of error.

The other definition is more recent. Frank Kermode defines it as a 'disconfirmation followed by a consonance; the interest of having our expectations falsified is obviously related to our wish to reach discovery by an unexpected route. It has nothing to do with our reluctance to get there at all. So that in assimilating the peripeteia we are enacting that readjustment of our expectations in regard to an end'. This points out the pleasure we receive from peripeteia which is quite different from the straightforward following of a narrative to its end, or in other words, mere change of fortune.

Having defined peripeteia and identified its characteristic pleasure, we must also consider what this pleasure actually consists of. This is the element of surprise or wonder [Gk. Thaumaston]. The source of wonder is often the tragic recognition or anagnorisis. Recognition has been variously defined. In Aristotle it is the recognition of persons through tokens, artistic contrivances, memory, reasoning (including false inferences) and lastly, arising out of the events themselves (as in Oedipus Rex). Aristotle defines this anagnorisis as a change from ignorance to knowledge. In terms of Humphrey House's analogy, it would mean the realization that you have got hold of the wrong end of the stick. House himself defines recognition thus, 'The discovery of the truth of the matter is the ghastly wakening from the state of the ignorance which is the very essence of hamartia.' Other scholars define it variously as 'a way in which the emotional potential... can be brought to its highest voltage, so to speak at the moment of discharge', or, 'recognition brings its illumination, which can shed retrospective light'.

Aristotle likes best the recognition which arises out of the events themselves, as in Sophocles's Oedipus Rex. The whole play is a step by step unravelling of Oedipus's true identity and Oedipus's holding the wrong end of the stick, as it were, in trying to discover his identity without knowing that the results will be catastrophic. At second best, he places those tragedies where reasoning effects the recognition. Together with these definitions, we could compare the slightly different angle from which Terence Cave views recognition. For him it is a stumbling block to belief which disturbs the decorum. From this comparison we realise the complicated nature of recognition. In the unravelling of the complex plot the point of the recognition is very different from that possible in a simple plot. The combination of peripeteia and recognition does not merely affect the characters in the tragedy. They can also extend to the audience or the reader. The unexpectedness of the tragic catastrophe which the complex plot brings [the element of wonder or thaumaston] heightens our feelings of pity and fear as well as other related emotions.

Here it would be useful to look at another famous assertion of Aristotle's. In Ch XIV of the *Poetics* he says, 'the pleasure which the poet should afford is that which comes from pity and fear through imitation'. Perhaps an examination of pity and fear together with imitation can give us a better idea of the pleasures incidental to tragedy. Let us start with an appraisal of pity and fear.

Pity and fear are man's sympathy for the good part of mankind in the bad part of their experiences. Pity is evoked when there is a discrepancy between the agent and Fate, and fear when there is a likeness between the agent and us. Stephen Dedalus defines Pity and Fear in James Joyce's *A Portrait of the Artist as a Young Man.* He calls pity the feeling which arrests the mind in the presence of whatsoever is grave and constant in human-sufferings and unites it with the human sufferer. Terror, or fear, is that which unites it with the secret cause..

Aristotle himself gives similar definitions of these terms in his *Rhetoric* [books V and II]. There he defines them as a species of pain. It is here that we can begin to consider the idea that tragic pleasure derives from the purgation of these emotions. The idea of purgation as a medical metaphor has been in vogue for a long time and can be substantiated by examples from Aristotle's *Problems* [problem XXX] where coldness of black bile accompanies 'despair and fear' and heat is the suggested cure which restores the temperature to a temperate mean. Aristotle, unlike his teacher Plato, says that the emotions are good in themselves.

Therefore there should be no need to purge the feelings of pity and fear. Instead, a more sensible definition of tragic pleasure would be that concomitant with the proper feeling of these emotions. By proper I mean a temperate attitude to these emotions as Aristotle teaches in his *Nichomachean Ethics.*

In Book II of his *Ethics*, he says: fear and confidence and appetite and anger and pity and in general pleasure and pain may be felt both too much and too little, and in both cases not well; but to feel them at the right times, with reference to the right objects, towards the right people, with the right motive, and in the right way, is what is both intermediate and best, and this is characteristic of virtue.

Aristotle's idea of the mean is derived from the Pythagoreans who applied it to music. Here we may note that another place where Aristotle uses the term catharsis is in his *Politics* and in the context of giving 'relief to overcharged feeling' through music. Interestingly, here too, he mentions pity and fear among the emotions dealt with and the restoration is once again to a temperate mean.

Is catharsis the only possible source of pleasure in tragedy? Humphry House does not think so. Those who are temperate in themselves and do not require an adjustment of their emotional reactions to tragic situations, still derive pleasure from tragedy. Even Plato in *The Republic* testifies to this fact: 'even the best of us enjoy it and let ourselves be carried away by our feelings; and are full of praises for the merits of the poet who can most powerfully affect us in this way.'. The pleasure arising out of poetry is therefore not entirely dependent on catharsis. Instead, it works in two ways. In Book VII [section 11 - 14] Aristotle discusses 'pure' pleasure and 'incidental' pleasure. The former is universal and is accompanied by no pain and is likened to the pleasure arising out of contemplation. Those who experience this do so solely by contemplating and appraising the imitation of human emotions in tragedy.

It is through this view that we bring our focus back on the last part of Aristotle's statement quoted above. Pleasure is effected through imitation [or mimesis]. As Aristotle said imitation is itself a pleasurable act. All of this applies to epic as well as tragedy and can probably be extended to other types of poetry. The specifically 'tragic' pleasure is that pertaining to the medium and the dramatic mode of tragedy. These constitute the specific imitative aspects of tragedy.

The idea of tragic pleasure therefore necessarily consists as Aristotle aptly puts it 'in that which comes with pity and fear through imitation'. A heightened sense of pity and fear is effected when the necessary and probable events take an unexpected turn. This is possible in the complex plot with the accompanying peripeteia and anagnorisis. Thus our examination of the elements of the complex plot has led us to a consideration of pity and fear. These together with imitation [or mimesis] help us understand the pleasure peculiar to tragedy.

Chapter 19

Imitation and Literature

Imitation is a foundational concept in the creation and study of literature. The fundamental assumptions embedded in imitation create a distinct and divisive method of perception. Imitation requires a basic belief in separation: appearance apart from reality, form apart from content. Literary works possess a dual existence, where the surface becomes most useful in its ability to reveal the substance contained within. Because the truth remains concealed, it can only be discerned or discovered through imitation. Thus imitation exists as an intermediary in a variety of artistic representations, each aspiring for an accurate depiction of meaning, perhaps even the basic truths of human existence. For Plato, however, art imitates a world that is already far removed from authentic reality, Truth, an inherently flawed copy of an already imperfect world. Art as an imitation is irrelevant to what is real. Many critics since Plato have attempted to reestablish the essential value of art by redefining or renegotiating the boundaries between imitation and authentic reality, between the text itself and meaning.

From ancient to more modern critics, art is defined, vilified, or redeemed by its ability to imitate. Aristotle values imitation as a natural process of humanity. Tragedy is simply a manifestation of the human desire to imitate. He asserts that every person "learns his lesson through imitation and we observe that all men find pleasure in imitations". Unlike Plato's world of Forms, knowledge of truth and goodness are rooted in the observable universe to Aristotle. Because imitation strives to create accurate particularized images of the real world, it is a source for potential discovery and delight. Neoclassical criticism accepts as givens Aristotle's statements about the nature of art and reality. Art is valuable precisely because it is imitative. As Sir Philip Sydney states, "Poesy is an art of imitation...with this end, to teach and delight" . Imitation not only entertains, but gains a moral/ethical purpose: to teach virtue. Artists must, in addition to possessing great creative skills, also bear moral responsibility for shaping their imitations. Samuel Johnson seems to revisit Plato's attack upon art with his admission that an accurate imitation of morally questionable subject matter is not only unacceptable, but potentially harmful to those who encounter it. In order to accommodate a strong moral sense, Johnson describes imitation as a process of interpretation. "The business of a poet... is to examine, not the individual, but the species...He must write as an interpreter of nature" . Imitation and the role of the imitator has evolved. Rather than an indiscriminate scribe copying an endless list of details both good and bad, each artist attempts to imitate the general qualities of humanity that promote goodness. Even within Romanticism, a writer like Wordsworth who challenges the literary styles and moral authority of preceding traditions, seeks to express his art by quietly imitating the inner, visceral, and emotional world of his own mind. Imitation is transformed into a deeply personal but ultimately universal experience, for Wordsworth "considers...the mind of a man as naturally the mirror of the fairest and most interesting qualities of nature".

Though definitions of imitation may have expanded in some eras or contracted in others, I would submit that most (if not all) Western literary criticism can be seen as an espousal of or reaction against the imitative function of art. Imitation, whether a work of art points toward an abstract truth or the subjective consciousness of an individual mind, presents a powerful theory of human communication. With its beginnings in Kant, Formalist criticism has surfaced as a response to mimetic assumptions about art and reality, insisting that the form of a text is inseparable from its meaning. Formalism does provide a counterpoint to representational art, but the boundaries of this debate have been determined in advance by the very notion of imitation. It may be, as Susan Sontag states, that "all Western consciousness of and reflection upon art have remained within the... theory of art as mimesis or representation" . The questions raised by imitation may well be integral and unavoidable in any literary or critical enterprise.

Aristotle in Africa: History, Fiction, and Truth in El Gallardo Español

El gallardo español is one of Cervantes's least known, little read, and most misunderstood plays. The few extant critical statements dealing with it address only its supposed "nationalist" spirit, its putative autobiographical resonances of Cervantes's North African experiences, its inscription of myth (De Armas), its historical verisimilitude and novelistic elements (Zimic), or the contrasting of myth, honor, and reality. While critics remain at odds as to the play's sense, however, the text itself offers its own explicit instructions regarding its purpose and meaning. In the closing statement to the audience, Guzmán, an actual historical personage inscribed in the text, observes in a metafictional gloss that it is time to end the play:

Cuyo principal intento
Ha sido mezclar verdades
Con fabulosos inventos .

The problematics of truth and fiction are, thus, according to one of the characters in the play essential to its understanding. This specific intentional statement, of course, leads us to one of the abiding concerns in all of Cervantes's works —the nature of fiction itself and its ability to depict and replicate the truth.

Using this specific declaration of intention as a point of departure, it is in fact possible to read *El gallardo* backward — that is, examine the text closely in light of its concluding statement and pursue those instances in it where Cervantes has sought to juxtapose fiction and truth. This reading strategy reveals that the play is primarily concerned with its own status as a fictional construct, and that Cervantes in writing it was responding to issues raised by contemporary critical theory. *El gallardo español,* it becomes clear, was conceived not just with the intention of forging a naive merger of fact and fiction, but to probe the limits, possibilities, and difficulties of integrating historical and strictly imaginative (essentially mendacious) discourses. In this way, it emerges as an early and profound Cervantine inquiry into the legitimacy of Aristotelian doctrine within a specifically dramatic context.

To begin to understand the significance of the closing lines of *El gallardo* it is necessary to turn to Chapter 48 of the first part of *Don Quijote* where, using the same terms, the Neo-Aristotelian *canónigo de Toledo* holds forth on the notion of the ideal *comedia,* from which "saldría el oyente alegre con las burlas, enseñado en las veras, admirado de los sucesos, discreto con las razones, advertido con los embustes, sagaz con los ejemplos, airado contra el vicio y enamorado de la virtud; que todos estos afectos ha de despertar la buena comedia en el ánimo del que la escuchare, por rústico y torpe que sea, y de toda imposibilidad es imposible dejar de alegrar y entretener, satisfacer y contentar, la comedia que todas estas partes tuviere.

Staged in a recent historical setting, the siege of the Spanish North African fortress of Oran in 1563, and doubtless based upon oral testimony as well as the events recorded in Luis de Mármol's *Descripción general de Africa* [Málaga, 1573], *El gallardo,* mimicking Neo-Aristotelian doctrine, purports to claim verisimilar legitimation through the invocation of historical referents.

Indeed, Canavaggio has traced the play's fidelity to history and how it reflects not only incidents up to the assault on Mersel-Kébir and the fortress of San Salvador, but the central role of D. Martín de Córdoba in the encounter, the heroics of D. Fernando de Cárcamo in the siege, the intervention of the Spanish military engineers in reinforcing the fortifications, and the final, unexpected arrival of the flotilla of D. Alvaro de Bazán, as well as the details of *razzia* warfare along the African frontier as reported by Braudel and other historians of Christian-Moslem conflicts in the sixteenth-century Mediterranean. The play's historical foundations and its explicit closing references to the constraints of Neo-Aristotelian theory seem to suggest that it is a programmatic implementation of the latter. Quite to the contrary, Cervantes appears to inscribe the Neo-Aristotelian model in order to test and subvert it. For example, the most noteworthy consideration in Cervantes's manipulation of history in *El gallardo* is not its fidelity to actual circumstances, or its adherence to particulars, but the very recent vintage of the events he portrays and their permutations in their textualization.

Although Tasso, in *Del poema eroico*, had counseled the invocation of history to persuade that the things treated by poets are worthy of belief and authority ("siano degne di fede e d'autorità", he went on to recommend that they confine their choice to historical occurrences in the distant past. Tasso did this because the poets' audience may know, or even have lived, the inscribed events and be enticed to point out inaccuracies in their representation. What, then, are we to make of Cervantes's use of the siege of Oran in *El gallardo*, and his evident departure from Neo-Aristotelian orthodoxy? Is the siege of Oran there to lend verisimilitude to the play, or is it, perhaps, there to provoke a subversion of the very authority of history itself and fly in the face of his Aristotelian contemporaries? These are some of the questions I wish to explore.

In his exploitation of the recent historical past Cervantes doubtless knew he ran the risk of confronting contradiction from his audience and that he should avoid, in Cascales' words "haver quien con vista de ojos se lo contradiga". Indeed, he elaborates upon just this point in a self-consciously theatrical episode of the *Persiles*, where two student dramatists professing to have been captives in North Africa are tempted to capitalize upon the recent historical past, and run headlong into living, contradictory witnesses of the events they seek to enact. *Historia* / history in the *Persiles* episode is judiciously transformed into *historia* / story, until a magistrate in the audience, himself a former captive in Africa, demands topographical details of Algiers which the performers fail to provide, thus exposing their play as a barefaced lie. They are, of course, denounced as prevaricators, but, invoking the virtue of justice tempered by mercy, they are finally forgiven by the magistrate for their dishonesty. More than mere entertainment, the episode of the bogus captives in the *Persiles*, with its deliberate representation of recent, easily contradictable historical events, serves a significant literary purpose in that it offers to a critical audience an opportunity to perceive the artificious uses of history in the construction of verisimilar texts, as it exposes the essential fictionality of the "true" events the captives allege to represent. So too in *El gallardo*.

El gallardo deconstructs its own claim to historical verisimilitude. The unmasking of its claim to historicity is registered repeatedly in the intrusive, overly emphatic, and parodic first person narrative interjections scattered in the play's stage directions. For example, prior to the introduction of Buitrago, a figure cut from the cloth of the *miles gloriosus* and the *gracioso* who offers his mediation on behalf of the souls in Purgatory, the stage notations indicate that he carries "una tablilla con demandas de las ánimas de purgatorio, y pide para ellas." They then go on to stress that "esto de pedir para las ánimas es cuento verdadero, que yo lo vi, y la razón por que pedía se dice adelante". Such a unique and vigorous narrative intervention punctuating the veracity of what is portrayed (and at the same time calling it a "cuento verdadero") in a discursive space customarily reserved in theatrical texts for the agentless passive voice, points more to the self-conscious awareness of the possibility of questioning the truth, and hence its instability, in what is represented.

These parenthetical narrative comments suggest an uneasiness —indeed, by their very presence, an invitation to contradict the text's certification of historical actuality and through their extravagance, deliberately draw our attention to the essential artificiality of the events being portrayed —to their radical textuality and detachment from the reality which the play purports to duplicate. The very gesture of invoking textual credibility and seeking to ratify the truth of Buitrago's portrait calls our attention to the fact that it, and everything else in *El gallardo,* is shaped by language and is in effect fictive. By its impertinent insistence that it contains some kind of specific verifiable link to an extratextual world, the play disrupts its own mechanism for constructing a viable willing suspension of disbelief. Indeed, it is at moments like this that we are led to question whether Cervantes ever meant *El gallardo* to be staged at all, and to consider the possibility that it was a drama destined solely to be read —an elaborate experiment in dramatic craft meant to invite a meditation upon the abiding Aristotelian question of the legitimacy of texts which profess to stage empirical historical truths.

Instead of seriously emphasizing the verisimilitude of the events, the anomalous parenthetical *ex abruptos* of *El gallardo* strike a discontinuous, humorous note. In fact, the commentary in these stage directions seems purposefully transgressive since it amusingly establishes the proximity of an authorial voice in the play and undermines its objectivity, as well as its theatricality and power of illusion. It is an unmistakable reminder of the play's artificiality, its fundamentally fictive constitution, and the creative imagination which has crafted it. At the same time, it proves a flagrant trespass of the Aristotelian precept that the poet, in El Pinciano's words, "deve hablar lo menos que él pueda" (*Philosophía antigua poética,* III, 208). It serves as a reminder that even eyewitness accounts professing to be historical are mediated authorial constructs ever incapable of adequately recuperating the past. While the Aristotelians presumptuously sought to affirm the mimetic autonomy of texts, in *El gallardo* Cervantes boldly questions their independence from within and asserts the author's persistent power over them.

As *El gallardo* parodies the Aristotelian claims to historical verisimilitude, it appropriates intentionally obtrusive imaginative elements and motifs from medieval romance, *romancero* balladry, and renaissance epic, further complicating through speech and action the problematics of the representation of the truth in language, text, and artifice. The transparent fictive antecedents of the noble Moor, the single combats, the amorous triangles, and the love quests, the chance encounters, the exotic disguises, and the stylized, ambiguous language of the play would all not have been lost upon its late sixteenth-century reader. They would, in fact, doubtless have led to a sense of teasing *déjà vu* and to a heightened awareness of the play's artificiousness. For example, Don Fernando de Saavedra, the gallant hero of the piece, while purporting to be modeled upon the historical Don Fernando de Cárcamo, is conspicuously reminiscent both in name and deed with the intrepid captive Sayavedra of the well-known "Río verde" ballads, which serve to close Part I of Pérez de Hita's *Guerras civiles de Granada,* not to mention the Sayavedra in other Cervantine works.

Similarly, the character Guzmán invokes resonances of other ballads and other legendary sieges (cf. the "Romance de don Henrique de Guzmán," Solalinde, 109-10; as well as the chronicle accounts of the deeds of Guzmán el Bueno), while the name of the Moorish heroine, Arlaxa, summons echoes of Lindaraxa (Pérez de Hita, 292-3), as well as one of the female protagonists from the popular sixteenth-century song, "Tres morillas me enamoran en Jaén". More importantly, however, the play's very title also flaunts its literary genealogy through an explicit reference to Ercilla's well-known epic, *La Araucana,* which invokes the prowess of an anonymous "gallardo español" during the siege of the fortress of Tucapel—a celebrated episode played out in Ercilla's text amidst his narrator's insistence upon the historical veracity of the incredible deeds he narrates:

Es cosa que en mil gentes han parado
y están en duda muchos hoy en día,
pareciéndoles que esto que he contado
es alguna ficción y poesía. . . (I, 164).

The resonances of *La Araucana* thus go deeper than superficial allusions to the feats of "el gallardo español" described in Canto II. In the latter, Ercilla introduces his own abiding concern with the Neo-Aristotelian tension of history and poetry in his text, emphatically championing the historical veracity of what is told there, and in this way foreshadows *El gallardo*'s engagement with the same themes. Cervantes's admiration for Ercilla is, of course, well-documented and unambiguously registered in Chapter VI of the first part of *Don Quijote,* where he includes *La Araucana* among three of "los mejores [poemas] que en verso heroico, en lengua castellana están escritos, y pueden competir con los más famosos de Italia" (I, 75). The origins of *El gallardo español* are hence steadfastly rooted in Cervantes's reading of Ercilla's poem, and reflect both his and humanism's broad-ranging preoccupation with the Neo-Aristotelian problematics of history and fiction in epic texts. Quite aside from its conspicuous references to romance, balladry, and vernacular epic, Cervantes's play is also richly allusive to classical textual antecedents and to the troublesome questions of history and poetry in them raised by their humanist readers and critics. Through a complex interplay of intertextual references, Cervantes places *El gallardo* squarely within the sixteenth-century Aristotelian debate on verisimilitude in ancient epic poetry. Not only is the siege of Oran meant to reflect contemporary history, it is expected to evoke another disputed historical siege portrayed in classical texts —the paradigmatic siege of Troy.

Cervantes explicitly signals his Trojan subtext when Alimuzel, at the walls of Oran, goads Don Fernando to single combat:

Y para darte ocasión
de que salgas mano a mano
de verte conmigo agora,
de estas cosas te hago cargo:
que peleas desde lejos,
que el arcabuz es tu amparo
que en comunidad aguijas
y a solas te vas despacio;
que eres Ulises nocturno,
no Telamón al sol claro .

There are, in fact, numerous, repeated references to Troy throughout the play: at other junctures, Oropesa, Arlaxa's

Christian captive, for example, compares his mistress to Medea , and Don Fernando to both Hercules and Hector .

The assault on the fortress of Tucapel in *La Araucana* is also shot through with echoes of the siege of Troy, including a Trojan-horse-like ruse used by the Indians to penetrate the stronghold. Cervantes's preoccupation with the tension between historical and poetic discourses in epic texts may thus have been conflated imaginatively in terms of both Homer and Ercilla—in terms of its manifestation in both ancients and moderns.

However, perhaps the most provocative allusion to Troy, and most significantly to Homer's critical reception of Aristotelian humanists, is found in Alimuzel's double death and double resurrection. In two instances, by both word and deed, he is slain —first by Buitrago and then by Don Fernando. In the first encounter, Alimuzel exclaims "¡Muerto soy; Alá me ayude!" while Arlaxa cries out "acude Lozano, acude, / que han muerto a tu grande amigo," as the stage direction says "Cae Alí dentro, y éntrase Arlaxa tras él" . In the second, Alimuzel reappears anew without explanation and Don Fernando strikes him down with his sword. Again, the Moor falls "dentro del vestuario" as he pronounces the words "¡Muerto me has, moro fingido / y cristiano mal cristiano" , just to rematerialize in the last scene of the play where Arlaxa gives him her hand, and where both he and his three lives pass in silence.

These episodes doubtless recall Priam's two deaths in the Homeric poems, which proved one of the polemical centerpieces of Renaissance literary theory. It is, in fact, Priam's double death (he is inexplicably killed twice by different antagonists in two different situations), as well as several other logical inconsistencies in Homer's poems, which led theorists to invoke repeatedly the Horatian topos of "aliquando bonus dormitat Homerus" (*Poetica,* 359), or the instances of "when good old Homer slept," to rationalize the Greek poet's infractions against historical verisimilitude.

The glaring puzzling events at the close of *El gallardo* lead the careful observer to marvel at them, though they are never satisfactorily explained. In fact, the Count of Alcaudete, properly astonished by all the discontinuities and transformations of the things he has witnessed in the last scene, points to them and exclaims with mock Aristotelian amazement "estoy tan suspenso, / porque de ellas veoel fin, / y no imagino el comienzo" , underscoring the very artificiousness of the dramatic conventions employed in the *comedia* of which he is a character. The count's remarks emphasize the indeterminacy of the play's closure and its ultimate non-compliance with Aristotelian precepts. Though the action has come to a final resolution, few can logically tell how it got there. In a droll comeback to the count's confusion, too, Don Fernando responds: "te lo diré a su tiempo" , the equivalent of "Trust me, I'll have to tell you later." Rather than stressing a finale rendering all that has transpired credible and comprehensible, the Count marks his bewilderment and consternation, his lingering desire for suitable believable explanations —which are never forthcoming. Though the threads of the action have been gathered together, they are clearly left more tangled than tied at the close of the play. With this in *El gallardo,* and with turns like Alimuzel's incredible double death, the construction of a rational, verisimilar whole comprising a feasible mimetic covenant between the author and an audience becomes unworkable. By calling attention to his forced denouement, the play itself tells us it has failed to achieve both formal coherence and willing suspension of disbelief, the seamless synthesis of *burlas* and *veras* lying at the centre of the Neo-Aristotelian ideal.

The dialectics of truth and fiction are inscribed in the play at a deeper level—at the level of language itself. The mediating nature of language is constantly highlighted, and the complications of envisioning it as transparent are sharpened through the play's ongoing inscription of lies. The self-conscious repetition of permutations on the word *mentir* saturates the text to the point of being obtrusive, as the characters rightly question the truth of all they see. Don Fernando, despite his gallantry, is in fact an inveterate liar, and his mendacity is ironically highlighted by Cervantes through one of the Count of Alcaudete's credulous remarks. In the closing scene, the count turns to the hero and says innocently: "siempre vuestras palabras / responden a vuestros hechos." To which Don Fernando replies: "entiende que ya no miento".

Indeed, all of the characters in the play, in one form or another, embrace some type of duplicity. But perhaps none is more interesting than Doña Margarita, who, cross dressed, appears suddenly in Oran not only as a man but then as a Moor, considerably complicating the instability of the representation of the truth in the ostensibly easy questions of gender and cultural identity. Her cross cultural cross dressing incarnates ambivalence, indeterminacy, and conjecture —the ongoing transfiguration of all that is seen and heard. A protean figure, Doña Margarita is something different to everyone she encounters. Both the characters in the drama and the observer outside of it are intentionally compelled to act as interpreters of the words as well as the deeds constituting the *comedia* and enter into the elaborate interplay of fiction and truth. Dialogues are constructed polysemously and produce a wealth of different resonances and echoes, cognizant of the power of speech to transfigure imaginatively surface appearances. Don Juan believes he recognizes his sister, the disguised Doña Margarita, yet he is told repeatedly she is the Moorish maiden Fátima. Cervantes ironically marks Don Juan's self-doubt and alarm at what he hears and sees through the equivocal use of the noun and the verb *mora*:

Por ser grande la distancia
que hay de mi hermana a ser mora,
imagino que en mí mora
gran cantidad de ignorancia.
Extraño es el devaneo
con quien vengo a contender,
pues no me deja creer
lo que con los ojos veo .

Finally, driven beyond Neo-Aristotelian *admiratio,* don Juan is farcically propelled to the edge of madness by the contradictions of all he perceives, exclaiming:

Que me admiro,
y en juicio me apoco.
Por dicha, ¿hace Mahoma
milagros?
Y hace transformaciones?

Facts themselves are destabilized, made relative and contingent, in *El gallardo* as they are related through language. The ambivalence of truth and lies resides at the level of words themselves and is demonstrated by alternating their transparency and opacity to produce calculated misreadings and misinterpretations. From our privileged ironic perspective, what is verbally fabricated is then visually denied; and what is physically embodied as real is subsequently verbally deconstructed. The persistence of speech and appearances which deceive the observer is insistently brought to our attention. The force of the subjectivity underpinning all notions of the truth is suggested by the fact that words and things are represented only in relation to the angle from which we and the characters in the play grasp them.

Through the ironic interplay of hearing, seeing, and believing, followed by radical disabuse, we are led to realise that the distinction between the factual and the fictive is really only one of hierarchy, never one of substance, and that it is difficult, if not impossible, to separate the two. By means of the extensive use of dramatic irony, and the construction of lies which define the links between all his characters, Cervantes toys with the notion that there is more than one way to compose truths.

Cervantes in *El gallardo* thus takes us beyond a facile Neo-Aristotelian convergence of history and poetry to the very threshold of the *Verfremdungseffekkt,* and to the calculated contemplation at all levels of the uncertainty of the actual and the fantastic. Through the overt utilization of stylized language and easily recognizable motifs from imaginative literature, particularly romance, balladry, and classical and vernacular epic, he sought to heighten the awareness of the ambivalence of both *burlas* and *veras* —to create moments of critical detachment from the play, in order to remind us that it was indeed just that a play not life but its textual representation. As he stated later in the "Adjunta al Parnaso," the intention behind publishing his plays in book form was "para que se vea de espacio lo que pasa apriesa, y se disimula, o no se entiende, cuando las representan" (Ed. Gaos, 183). His goal was thus not to make *burlas* indistinguishable from *veras*, but to signal their kinship in dramatic texts, and render an evaluation of theater itself by exposing and manipulating the very devices through which it creates illusions and purports to represent reality. In this way, *El gallardo* offers a kind of ontological critique of theater which discloses at every step the semiotic strategies it exploits to represent the truth.

The play organizes a confrontation between self-consciously fictive and historical discourses in order to highlight the effacement of the boundaries between the two and place into question linguistic and textual referentiality, leading us ultimately to a *mise en abîme*. The troublesome cohabitation of *veras* with undisguised *burlas* unmasks the way dramatic texts seek to create real-seeming illusions and, from beginning to end, through its artificiousness, ambiguous language, the intrusion of extradiegetic commentary and even a point of view in the stage directions, the names and allusive identities of the characters and what occurs to them, there is a consistent attempt to convey the sense of a fictional world, a construct, set up against a background of well-known historical facts. Even the truth on stage is disguised, distorted, and transformed as we, along with the characters, are led to ponder the nature of what we hear and behold and formulate conclusions about it just to be denied, contradicted, and confounded in the end. As in his best known dramatic pieces exploring the nature of theater (*Pedro de Urdemalas* and *El retablo de las maravillas*), in *El gallardo* Cervantes gathers all the artifices of the stage and integrates them into a structure that constantly calls attention to them and to their persistent counterfeit of truth. Although the play's concluding statement parallels the Neo-Aristotelian canon's agenda for the ideal theater in *Don Quijote* (I, 48), a retrospective reading of *El gallardo* underscores Cervantes's awareness of verisimilitude's abiding fictionality —his questioning of it and his final refusal to yield simplistically to the Neo-Aristotelian programme.

If *El gallardo* was in fact written as early as 1594, as Cotarelo y Valledor claims, it is perhaps Cervantes's earliest critical response to the paradoxes posed by Neo-Aristotelian aesthetics and deserves our careful scrutiny. Whatever its date of composition, however, it is clear that the play illustrates far more than a clever excursion into the *comedia nueva* (Marrast, 61) or a slavish imitation of Neo-Aristotelian fashion. In its quest to merge *burlas* with *veras* it ultimately undermines the very possibility of ever reconciling the two, calling into question the capacity of texts to represent empirical truths. As it does this, it interrogates the very critical abstractions which provoked its composition. As in all of Cervantes's work, *El gallardo* is at once a creative and self-scrutinizing gesture which confronts the very theoretical underpinnings upon which it rests and, ultimately, the foundations of writing itself. *El gallardo* does, in fact, partially accomplish the artistic goals set out by the canon of Toledo for the theater—to instruct and to entertain. However, in its interrogation of verisimilitude, and its awareness of itself as a text, it constitutes a departure from them and designates one more profound Cervantine inquiry into the ability of language to fabricate illusions.

In the Poetics

Aristotle presents the principles of artistic composition. While the work treats many forms of imaginative creation, including comedy, epic, dialogue, and even music and dance, it focuses most particularly on the elements of tragedy.

Textual History

Little is known about the fate of Aristotle's works after his death. It is believed by some scholars that for about two hundred years following his death, the works were either lost or hidden. They were discovered by Sulla (138-78 B.C.) and brought to Rome. According to one prominent scholar, Lane Cooper, the *Poetics* dates from some time prior to 323 B.C. Cooper comments that the *Poetics* is perhaps a version of

Aristotle's lecture notes, or perhaps even a collection of notes transcribed by someone who attended Aristotle's lectures on the subject. Modern editions of Aristotle's works derive from Roman editions dating back to the late first century b.c. In the Middle Ages, Latin and Arabic translations broadened the influence of Aristotle's teachings, although, as Marvin Herrick has noted, the translations available in England during this time were often thought to be of poor quality. By the end of the fifteenth century, however, Greek versions of the text of the *Poetics* were available in Italy, and Englishmen traveled there to study it. From that point on, Aristotle's views on the poetic art gained and lost influencein various periods, but gradually became a significant force in the criticism of poetry, drama, and literature.

Critical Reception

Just as Aristotle devotes most of his attention in *Poetics* to tragedy, modern scholars dedicate much of their critical energy to evaluating Aristotle's views on tragedy. In the English translation of Aristotle's definition, tragedy is an "imitation" of a "serious and complete" action, with a "definite magnitude," or theme, that is "humanly significant." Tragedy employs "pleasing language" or "enhanced utterance;" it is characterized by action rather than narration; and it achieves "through pity and fear" what is known as "catharsis" or "purgation." A major issue of critical debate is this concept of imitation. Often, critics attempt to answer the question of what is to be imitated, and in doing so, defend the concept of dramatic imitation against the negative connotation of an imitation being less pure or noble than the original. John W. Draper has noted that while "imitation" has often been misunderstood, it should be conceived of as art's imitation of nature, where nature is understood to be the "creative force of the universe." Charles Sears Baldwin has discussed the Aristotelian concept of imitation as the representation of the character, emotions, and actions of men. Like Draper, Laurence Berns has argued that by imitation Aristotle meant the imitation of nature. Berns goes on to explain that not only is art to imitate what is "actual in nature," but the perfection that is potential in nature as well. Norman Gulley has taken a position similar to Baldwin's by maintaining that art represents human behaviour and its moral aspects.

Critics also grapple with other aspects of Aristotle's definition of tragedy, especially the role of catharsis. Catherine Lord has explained that to Aristotle, tragedy was a "goal-directed system," with the goal being catharsis. G. S. Brett has examined this goal, noting that the Greek term infers purgation and purification.

Brett has also stressed that Aristotle's definition of tragedy makes no reference to the effects to be experienced by spectators, and suggests that purgation is essential to tragedy without an audience to undergo the catharsis. Berns, on the other hand, maintains that the catharsis Aristotle describes is, in effect, a moral purification in which audience members or readers are taught what to fear and what to pity.

Another major source of debate among critics is Aristotle's emphasis on the primacy of plot over all other elements of tragedy. Catherine Lord has quoted the *Poetics* as stating that "without action there cannot be a tragedy; there may be without character." After noting that many critics resist this notion that character is entirely subordinate to plot, Lord has argued that in fact all issues related to character are a function of plot. Lord discusses the concept of *hamartia* as a function of plot as well, maintaining that while this word is often interpreted as the hero's tragic flaw, it is in fact a "simple mistake," not a moral frailty. Colin Hardie, however, has contended that plot and character are inseparable within the context of Aristotle's entire theory of poetics, even though parts of the *Poetics* seem to identify an antithesis between plot and character. Hardie explains that within the drama, the "facts and circumstances" through which character becomes defined are the plot. It is in an effort to "guarantee the individuality of character," Hardie maintains, that Aristotle emphasizes the significance of plot.

Aristotle's treatment of tragedy, combined with his coverage of other poetic arts, has contributed to the lasting significance of this treatise. The work has greatly influenced the development of literary criticism and continues to be regarded, in the words of Lane Cooper, as "one of the most illuminating and influential books ever produced by the sobre human mind."

No one can turn over the pages of The Harvard Classics without realizing how much of the most delightful writing of the last three hundred years has taken the form of the essay. No literary form is more flexible than this, and no form except lyric poetry has touched upon a wider variety of topics. Yet there is one subject of enduring human interest to which essayists are perpetually turning, and upon which they always find something new to say. It is the subject of Books and Reading. In the essays which deal with this perennially interesting topic, there is a constant expression of literary judgments—judgments that convey racial and national convictions, the ruling ideas of a generation or a school, or the likes and dislikes of individuals. These judgments, properly collected and classified, become the material for a history of literary criticism. Indeed, a surprisingly large proportion of the epoch-making documents of criticism are really essays, both in form and mood.

Importance of the Essay in Literary Critcism

The significance of the essay in the formation and perpetuation of critical doctrine is also apparent if one turns to the formal histories of criticism. Systematic treatises on the theory of the fine arts, including literature, have appeared at intervals since the time of Aristotle. The science of æsthetics, as we know it, was developed in Germany during the latter half of the eighteenth century, and it forms an integral portion of the philosophical system of Kant and of many other philosophers.

But these formal treatises upon the nature of beauty, involving as they do the analysis of the beautiful as it exists in the natural world and in works of art, appeal primarily to a few thinkers and scholars, and not to the general public. It is true that men of genius like Goethe, Schiller, and Burke have the faculty of discussing the philosophic basis of æsthetic theories in such a way as to make them interesting and highly instructive to the general reader. But as a rule the systematic treatises upon the nature and history of the fine arts, and of literature in particular, have been necessarily addressed to a limited audience. The discussions which have really caught the ear of the public have been the casual utterances of brilliant men in the act of attacking or defending a literary creed, of writing a preface to a book or a play, or of hazarding, in some dialogue, pamphlet, or essay, a new opinion about beauty, a new theory of poetry or of prose.

What is an Essay?

To understand, therefore, the history of actual critical opinion, one must study the essay. It is a very variable, highly personalized literary form: resembling now a dinner-table monologue or dialogue, and now a letter to a friend. Here it is a mere sparkling fragment of some solid mass of philosophical theory, and there it is a tiny jewel of paradox, interrogation, or fancy; here an echo of some great historical debate over tragedy or comedy, and there the first faint stirring of some new, living idea, which by and by will be tossed about with all the winds of doctrine.

But however changeable this literary type may be, one who reads the various essays in The Harvard Classics can hardly fail to get a general notion of the nature of "the essay." The type will gradually make itself clear to him, as something different from the formal treatise, the dialogue or the letter or the magazine article. He will learn to watch the type emerge into clear outline with Montaigne and Bacon. He will see that it modifies itself under the influence of national traits or of the fashions of successive historical periods, that it differentiates itself into species and varieties, precisely as other literary types undergo variation and development under specific conditions. It will flourish in one age and decline in another, as do the drama and the lyric, although, like them, the essay represents a certain permanent mood which never goes wholly out of fashion.

The Critical Essay

The reader who is interested in literary criticism will soon find that the essay has been a particularly convenient form for conveying literary theories from one mind or age to another. The "critical essay," while conforming in general to the flexible laws of "the essay," is used for a specific purpose. It deals with the emergence, continuance, and disappearance of critical opinions; it records, in an informal but none the less effective manner, the judgment of Europe upon books. Let us take a specific example. Charles Lamb's "Essay on the Tragedies of Shakespeare" is a singularly perfect specimen of "the essay" type.

It is personal and casual. It opens with the sentence: "Taking a turn the other day in the Abbey, I was struck with the affected attitude of a figure, which I do not remember to have seen before, and which upon examination proved to be a whole-length of the celebrated Mr. Garrick"; and then Lamb passes, with apparent artlessness, from the affectations and tricks of actors to the profound question of the possibility of an adequate representation of the personalities of Hamlet and Lear upon the stage. This personal essay, with its odd whims and fancies, deepens page by page into a masterly critical essay, which makes a distinct phase of the attitude of the English mind toward England's greatest poet.

In similar fashion, Victor Hugo's preface to his drama "Cromwell" is a capital example of a personal essay—an essay "rampant" in its defence of the author's own literary creed. But that creed as it happens, becomes also the triumphant creed of the young French Romanticists. They rallied around the preface to "Cromwell" as soldiers rally around a flag, and the essay became a concrete embodiment of a new reaction against Classicism, a significant document in the literary history of modern Europe.

National Character in the Essay

The two essays which have just been mentioned—personal in their immediate character, and yet even more significant as representing doctrines which came to be held by a generation or a school—may also serve to illustrate a third aspect from which essays may be regarded. One may study them, in chronological order, as successive indications of a national point of view. Thus the English critical essay, in the Elizabethan period, in the seventeenth century, or in any subsequent epoch, reveals the precise extent to which the English mind accepts, modifies, or rejects the main body of European critical doctrine. As affording material for such a chronological study, it is not essential that any particular English critical essay should be marked by personal distinction of style, or by special critical acumen. The undistinguished mass of book reviews, of gossip about writers, about the stage and other forms of contemporary art, is often the most valuable evidence of the instinctive working of the English mind. What does an average bookish Englishman, in a given decade, understand by the words "tragic," "comic," "heroic," "the unities," "wit," "taste," "humour," "Nature"? The historian finds the answer in a thousand casual expressions, each one of which bears the stamp of the period and the race. The Englishman interprets the general laws and phrases of European criticism in terms of his own neighborhood and time, and a collection of English critical essays thus illustrates the traits of the English national character.

The History of the Word "Essay"

Let us now turn from the broader relations of the essay with criticism, and endeavor to ascertain precisely what the word "essay" means. The older English form of the word is "assay," i. e., a trial or experiment. It is derived, through the French, from a late Latin word "exagium," which means a standard weight, or more precisely, the act of weighing. The word "examine" comes from the same Latin root. As defined by the "Century Dictionary," "essay" means I, A trial, attempt or endeavor; an experimental trial or test; an assay or test of metal. In literature, a discursive composition concerned with a particular subject, usually shorter and less methodical and finished than a treatise; a short disquisition. Dr. Samuel Johnson, who was himself one of the most famous essayists of his day, defines "essay" in his Dictionary as "A loose sally of the mind; an irregular indigested piece; not a regular and orderly composition." Possibly it was the Doctor's happy word "sally" which suggested to a recent writer, Mr. F. N. Zabriskie, the following excellent definition: "The essay is properly a collection of notes, indicating certain aspects of a subject, or suggesting thoughts concerning it; ... not a formal siege, but a series of assaults, essays or attempts upon it." It is for this reason that Mr. Zabriskie calls the essayist the excursionist of literature, the literary angler, the meditator rather than the thinker; and he points out that the German mind is not adapted to the essay, since the Germans are not satisfied to make mere assaults upon a subject, mere excursions into it; they must go through a subject from end to end and leave it a conquered territory.

The First Modern Essayists

Montaigne, who was the initiator of the modern essay (1580), laid stress upon its essentially autobiographic nature. He confesses that he writes "not to discover things, but to lay open myself." He thinks that an essay should be spontaneous and free from every artificial trammel. It should have the characteristics of open, varied, wide-ranging talk: "I speak unto paper as unto the first man I meet." Lord Bacon, whose first edition of essays appeared in 1597, is more orderly than Montaigne. He masses his material more closely, keeps to his topic, packs his sentences as full as they will hold. He is too austere for the leisurely, personal method of Montaigne; he imparts his concentrated worldly wisdom coolly, almost impassively; he loves the pregnant opening and close. "To write just treatises," he says, "requireth time in the writer and leisure in the reader, which is the cause that hath made me choose to write certain brief notes, set down rather significantly than curiously, which I have called *essays;* the word is late, but the thing is ancient. For Seneca's Epistles to Lucilius, if one mark them well, are but essays—that is, dispersed meditations." And finally, Addison, whose essays sum up the early eighteenth century as completely as Montaigne and

Bacon represent the late Renaissance, is quite as explicit as they are in emphasizing the informal character of this type of literature: "When I make choice of a subject that has not been treated on by others, I throw together my reflections on it without any order or method, so that they may appear rather in the looseness and freedom of an essay, than in the regularity of a set discourse."

The Antiquity of the Essay

The thing is ancient"; there is no doubt of that. Analogies to the mood of the modern essay and to its urbane, free, flexible methods of discussion, may be found in the "Dialogues" of Plato, in the "Lives" and "Morals" of Plutarch, in the letters of Cicero, Horace, and the younger Pliny, in the gossipy "Attic Nights" of Aulus Gellius, in the talks of Epictetus and the Meditations of Marcus Aurelius. There is nothing new under the sun; and there were Greek and Roman gentlemen quite as capable as Montaigne of writing with frankness, ease, quaintness, and an open-minded attitude of skeptical inquiry. But though they often revealed the spirit of the modern essayist, they were groping uncertainly after the appropriate literary form. Montaigne's great achievement was to hazard his fortunes in an unsurpassed series of "sallies," "assaults," "assays" upon a hundred entrenched topics, and always to come bravely off—so that his tactics became the model for all literary skirmishes. To think and feel and write like Montaigne was to produce the modern essay. Without his example, it is doubtful if we should have had the essays of Lamb, of Emerson, and of Stevenson.

Effect of The Renaissance on the Essay

Supporting the whole theory and practice of Montaigne, undoubtedly, stood the Renaissance itself. This "re-birth" of the human mind, this new awakening of vital energies and intellectual powers, involved a new way of looking at the world. Nothing seemed quite the same as it had been. Church and empire and feudal system were apparently weakening; new nationalities, new languages were to be reckoned with;

new continents were explored, new inventions altered the face of daily life; a new intellectual confidence, inquiry, criticism, supplanted the mediæval obedience to authority. There was a new "weighing," "assaying" of all things. The actual world was changing before men's eyes, and the inner world changed no less. There was universal curiosity about individual capacities and opinions, experiences and tastes. The whole "undulating and various" scheme of things—to use a favourite expression of Montaigne—was a direct provocative of the essay state of mind; and the essay form, in turn, in its looseness, vagueness, and range, was singularly adapted to the intellectual spirit of the period.

The Bookish Essay

One type of Renaissance essay, for example, concerned itself with a casual survey of the fragments of the classical and mediæval world. Modern books like Taylor's "Classical Heritage of the Middle Ages," and "The Mediæval Mind," Einstein's "Italian Renaissance in England," Sir Sidney Lee's "French Renaissance in England," Spingarn's "Literary Criticism in the Renaissance," and Saintsbury's "History of Criticism" set before us, with abundance of detail, the kind and extent of knowledge of the past which was possessed by Renaissance essayists. Caxton's naïve Prologues and Epilogues to the popular classical and mediæval books which he issued in English, Sir Philip Sidney's chivalrous "Defence of Poesy," and Edmund Spenser's explanation to Sir Walter Raleigh of the purpose of "The Faërie Queene" are good illustrations of the attitude of typical Englishmen toward the imaginative life of the past. Gregory Smith's collection of "Elizabethan Critical Essays" affords a fairly complete view of the critical ideas which sixteenth-century England had inherited from Europe. The evolution of the English critical essay, during the three hundred years which have elapsed since then, is mainly the story of the preservation of these ideas and their modification or transformation under the successive impacts of new intellectual forces, and of differing social and literary conditions.

The Essay as Expressive of Curiosity About Life

Another type of essay, originating in the Renaissance, and a favourite with Montaigne, deals not so much with books as with life itself. The new culture, the novel intellectual perceptions, altered at once the accepted theories of man's duty and destiny. Montaigne does not dogmatize about these matters: he asks questions, he suggests possible answers. The speculative essay, the philosophical and scientific essay, the social essay which draws its materials from the ever-renewed revelation of the actual life of man, all find their source in an awakened curiosity.

The enthusiasm, the gusto, with which sixteenth-century men discussed every topic within their range of vision, has remained an integral element of the effective essay. A man may set himself sadly and grimly to work upon his formal treatise, and write it through to the end with disillusion in his soul. But the born essayist, though knowing well enough that his raids into unconquered territory must be merely a perpetual series of sallies and retreats, nevertheless advances gayly to the assault. Like Lamb and Stevenson, he preaches without being a preacher; like Huxley and Tyndall, he teaches when he means only to inform; so communicable and infectious is this gift of curiosity about life.

The Autobiographical Essay

There is a third type of essay, originating in the Renaissance emphasis upon individualism, and confidently asserting itself upon the pages of Montaigne, Addison, Hazlitt, De Quincey, Emerson, Thoreau and a hundred other men. It is the autobiographic, "egotistic" essay—in which there is rarely any insolence of egotism, but only an insatiable curiosity about oneself, and an entire willingness to discuss that question in public.

If you like the man who is talking, this kind of essay is the most delightful of all. But it betrays a great deal, and like lyric verse—the most intensely personalized mode of poetry—it sometimes betrays too much. When the right balance is struck between openness and conceit, or when, as with

Emerson, the man is sweet and sound to the core, the self-revealing essay justifies itself. Indeed, it is thought by some critics that the subjective or lyrical quality of the essay is a part of its essential character. Thus Professor A. C. Bradley has asserted: "Brevity, simplicity, and singleness of presentation; the strong play of personality, the subjective charm, the delicate touch, the limited range of theme and of treatment, and the ordered beauty through exclusion of all disordered moods and fiercer passions—these flow directly from the presence and dominance of the lyrical element, and these are the constant features of the Essay."

One should add, perhaps, that all three of the essay types here touched upon—the "critical," the "ethical" or "philosophic," and the "personal"—were strongly coloured during the Renaissance, as they have been at intervals ever since, by the spirit of nationalism.

French criticism, in the sixteenth century as in the nineteenth, is very French. English criticism, in Dryden and Arnold, is very English; the moralizing of Milton's tractates and of Samuel Johnson's "Lives of the Poets," the personal assertiveness of Thoreau's essay on "Walking," and Lowell's essay on "Democracy" bear the unmistakable accents of England and of America. Blood tells, in the essay as elsewhere.

Essays as Historical Documents

In fact, one of the most interesting studies made available through The Harvard Classics is the survey of various national moods in successive historical periods. Take, for instance, the English essayists of the eighteenth century. Here are characteristic utterances of men so differently yet richly endowed as Addison and Swift, Steele and Defoe, Sidney and Samuel Johnson, Hume and Burke, yet the student of the eighteenth century, whether he is reading Hume or Burke on Taste, or Johnson explaining the plan of his great Dictionary, Defoe's ironical scheme for ridding the world of Dissenters, or Addison's delicately sentimental musings in Westminster Abbey, detects, beneath all the differences in style and varieties of personal opinion, the unmistakable traits of race, nation, and period. These essays are thus historical documents of high importance. One understands better, for reading them, the England of Marlborough and of Walpole, the England of the Pitts and the four Georges. Any one century, as Carlyle said long ago, is the lineal descendant of all the preceding centuries, and an intelligent reading of the English essays of the seventeenth, eighteenth, and nineteenth centuries is one of the best ways of learning that significant lesson.

Aristotle and the Critical Essay

Even if the reader of these essays has no special knowledge of English history, and has hitherto paid but little attention to the influence of one school of thought upon its successors, he cannot help discovering one difference between what we have called "the essay" and its more specialized from "the critical essay." "The essay" moves in a circle. Its orbit tends to return perpetually upon itself.

One may even say that the type was already complete in Montaigne, and that since then it has made no real advance; that we have only a succession of essayists, doing, of course with infinite personal varieties of pattern, precisely what Montaigne showed them how to do. But the critical essay advances, albeit by zigzag lines. It is obliged to tack, as the winds of doctrine shift and the tides of opinion ebb and flow, yet it is always steering, and not merely drifting. Take, for example, the most famous critical essay of the Greeks, the "Poetics" of Aristotle.

It is an attempt to establish certain fundamental principles of æsthetic criticism, such as the laws of epic poetry and the nature of tragedy. It analyzed the structure of contemporary works of literary art, tested the psychological effect of poem and play upon the mind of the reader and spectator, and laid down some shrewd rules for the guidance of poets. It is an essay rather than an exhaustive treatise, but it is by no means the sort of essay which Montaigne would have written had he been a Greek. It is impersonal, analytical, scientific. And so logical is its matter, so penetrating its insight, that it became a model of sound critical procedure.

The "rules" of Aristotle, based as they were upon the facts of human nature and the character of the literature of his day, deserved the reverence with which they were treated by the men who rediscovered them in the Renaissance. Trouble came only when the attempt was made to apply them rigidly and mechanically to poems and dramas of a type different from anything that Aristotle had known.

Yet out of this very confusion and necessity for readjustment came the "critical essay" as we know it. Aristotle had set up Truth as his beacon mark: Truth to the physical and psychological facts, to the laws of beauty which are also laws of the mind. When the critics of the Renaissance and of the age of Neo-Classicism in France and England, confronted as they were by new facts, tried loyally to adjust the Aristotelian formulæ to the writings of Tasso, Shakespeare, and Molière, they made queer work of it.

They endeavored to keep in mind both "the polestar of the ancients" and the "rules of the French stage among the moderns," to say nothing of the cross currents of actual contemporary fact. It was a difficult course to sail, and it is no wonder that the history of the critical essay exhibits every variety of daring or faltering seamanship. But the beacon mark of Truth was there all the while, and though no navigator has ever succeeded in beating quite up to it, it is reward enough for the critical essayist if he seems to be making headway.

Critical Tradition and the Essay

The writer of the critical essay, in short, finds that his course has been laid out for him by the very nature of the task which he has undertaken. The mere essayist, as we have seen, can sail in a circle, starting and ending with his own fancies; but the man who uses the essay as the vehicle of criticism must use chart and compass; must proceed from a given starting point to a definite point of arrival.

And he cannot do this if he is ignorant of the efforts of his predecessors, and unaware of the general aims and methods of critical procedure. If he is writing, for instance, on the theory of poetry, he does not wish to leave the matter where he found it: he desires to make, if he can, a contribution to that branch of human knowledge. But he is not likely to succeed unless he has a tolerably clear notion of just how far the world-old discussion has proceeded at the point where he himself takes up the debate.

When Horace wrote that clever versified essay on the poet's art, an essay which has been irreverently termed "the business man's guide to poetry," he had no intention of slavishly imitating the rules of the Greek theorists. But after all, his father had sent him to a Greek University, and the ghosts of his old professors were peeping over his shoulders as he wrote. And when, long afterward, the Italian Vida and the Frenchman Boileau came to write their own verse essays on the same topic, the ghost of the clever Roman held their pens. Sidney and Shelley, in composing their eloquent Defences of Poetry, had probably no conscious thought of continuing the formal discussion of poetic theory which the Greeks began and the Renaissance resuscitated; nevertheless, their confessions of faith in poetry form an essential chapter in the evolution of criticism.

So with the prefaces of Wordsworth and Coleridge and Walt Whitman. These men are innovators in theory and practice of their craft, but, like most of the successful innovators and "modernists" in art, they possessed a fairly accurate knowledge of the ancient defenses which they were trying to carry by assault. Yet these assaults, no matter how brilliant, never really end the siege. The final truth escapes complete analysis and definition. The history of the critical essay shows only a series of approximations, a record of endeavors which must be constantly renewed.

Types of Criticism

Out of all this variety of effort, however, three tendencies of criticism emerge. They are usually called the "judicial," the "interpretative," and the "impressionistic." The theoretical distinction between these tendencies of criticism is clear enough. "Judicial" criticism passes judgment upon established facts. It deals primarily with rules, with the "canons" of criticism, although it may, of course, examine the principles upon which these rules are based. Its estimates are likely to be dogmatic and magisterial.

It says bluntly, in the voice of Jeffrey, that Wordsworth's "Excursion" "will never do"; that his "White Doe of Rylstone" is "the very worst poem we ever saw imprinted in a quarto volume." It declares, with Professor Churton Collins, that "Criticism is to literature what legislation and government are to states." The aim of "interpretative" criticism, on the other hand, is not so much to pass judgment upon a specific work, as to explain it. It seeks and establishes, if possible, correct texts; it makes clear the biographical and historical facts essential to an understanding of the work in question. It finds and reveals the meaning and beauty there contained. It points out the ethical and social significance of the literary product. To explain a book, no doubt, is often tantamount to judging it; for if the book be demonstrated to be full of corruption, that is the most effective way of declaring it a corrupt book. Nevertheless, the object of the "interpretative" or "appreciative" critic is primarily expository, and he prefers that the reader himself should pass ultimate judgment, in the light of the exposition which has been made.

He puts the needful facts before the jury, and then rests his case. Sainte-Beuve is a master of this sort of criticism, as Jeffrey is of the magisterial. The "impressionistic" critic, finally, does not concern himself overmuch with the canons. He leaves "universal considerations" and "the common sense of most" to his rivals.

Textual criticism bores him. The examination of principles strikes him as too "scientific," the massing of biographical and historical details seems to him the work of the historian rather than the critic. He deals frankly in his own "impressions," his personal preferences, the adventures of his soul in the presence of masterpieces. He translates the sensations and emotions which he has experienced in his contact with books into symbols borrowed from all the other arts and from the inexhaustible stores of natural beauty.

His rivals may call him a man of caprice rather than a man

of taste, but they cannot really confute him, for such are the infinitely varied modes of physical and psychological reaction to the presence of the beautiful, that nobody knows exactly how the other man feels. We must take his word for it, and the words of impressionistic criticism have often been uttered with an exquisite delicacy and freshness and radiance that make all other types of literary criticism seem for the moment mere cold and formal pedantries.

The Union and Merging of Types of Criticism

So much for the theoretical distinction between the three tendencies. But no one can read many pages of the masters of modern criticism without becoming aware that all three tendencies frequently reveal themselves in the same man, and even in the same essay. Some of the famous "impressionists," like Lamb, Stevenson, Lemaître, and Anatole France, know a great deal more about the "canons" than they wish at the moment to confess. They play so skillfully with the overtones of criticism because they know the fundamental tones so well. Stevenson attempts "scientific" criticism in his essay on "Style," "historical" criticism in his essay on Pepy Jeffrey occasionally writes "national character" criticism quite in the expository method of Sainte-Beuve. Coleridge and Emerson, Arnold and Ruskin, 27 are too many-sided and richly endowed men to limit their literary essays to any one type of criticism.

The justification of this eclecticism of practice is found, as we have tried to show, in the nature of the essay itself. It is the most sinuous, varied, and individualized of all the forms of prose litera ure.

The moment it begins to deal with critical theory, however, it is obliged to make its reckoning with some one more of the processes of judgment which have been evolved in the history of the race; it tends then to become "historical," "scientific," "expository," "judicial"; it sails, as we have said, by the chart, instead of in the capricious circle of purely personal preferences. And it is in this relation of "the essay" to "the critical essay" that we discover something of the literary and social significance of essay writing.

It meets a need of the individual, and performs at the same time a function for society. The individual reader turns to the essayists for delight, for stimulus, for consolation, for a fortification of the will. Cicero and Montaigne and Thoreau will talk to him about friendship and books and behaviour. What more can he ask for? He finds in the essayists, as in the lyric poets, the reflection of his own moods, his own tastes, his own varied contact with experience.

In their company, as in the company of every form of art, he becomes intimately aware of the fullness and richness of life. As for society at large, the essayists—and particularly those who have occupied themselves with criticism—have aided in the establishment of standards of judgment. These standards are impersonal and relatively stable. They alter somewhat, it is true, with the progress of civilization, and with the temper of successive historical periods in each of the civilized races of the world.

But for any one generation the "norm" exists. The departures from it and the returns to it constitute the æsthetic and intellectual activity of that generation. Expansion and contraction, the study of mankind followed by the study of individual men and women; then a new series of generalizations followed by another series of concrete applications of ideas to life—that is the history of culture. And while "the essay" has from time to time asserted the claims of liberty in all matters of the mind, "the critical essay" has with equal persistence recognized and maintained the claims of authority.

One generation needs, no doubt, that its literary skirmishes should fight mainly on the side of freedom, and another generation will need no less that they should rally to the defence of law. There can be little doubt of the primary need of our own generation in America. We shall find most profit in reading those essayists who have a respect for literary standards, who are on the side of law.

Aristotle's Method And Place In Intellectual History

Aristotle's method, in ethics as in all other fields, was

critical and empirical. In the study of any subject he began by collecting, analyzing, and grouping all relevant facts in order to determine their meaning and relations with each other, and this gave him a systematic and factually correct basis from which to generalize about underlying rules or principles. In generalizing, he used either the inductive approach, reasoning from many observed single instances to a universal proposition, or the syllogism, a means of deductive reasoning which he invented, and defined as "certain things being stated, something else follows of necessity without need of further testimony," i.e., proceeding from previously established general rules or facts down to particular instances. The syllogism is used frequently by Aristotle in analytical sections of the *Nicomachean Ethics*. It has two premises—one major (universal) and the other minor (particular), and in its simplest form works as follows:

Major Premise: All A is B or: All men are mortal.
Minor Premise: C is part of A Socrates was a man.
Conclusion: C is B Socrates was mortal.

Of course, as Aristotle frequently warned, it is possible to reason correctly from false premises, thus coming up with a logically correct but untrue conclusion, and therefore it is of essential importance to make certain that the premises of a syllogism are true and sufficiently comprehensive to cover all cases.

These modes of reasoning illustrate the most significant difference between the Platonic and Aristotelian systems. Plato postulated the existence of ideal, absolute standards and forms, against which all human things had to be measured. Aristotle, while not specifically denying the existence of these abstract standards, approached the same questions from another direction, and tried to determine the nature of things by empirical observation and logical analysis, never stating a hypothesis without first testing it against the data.

Aristotle's work and method have had an unparalleled influence on the development of thought. In the Middle Ages he was considered an absolute authority on nearly every subject, referred to by Saint Thomas Aquinas as "The

Philosopher" and by Dante as "Master of those that know," although much of Aristotle's insistence on empirical method was ignored by his medieval disciples.

Aristotle's technique and influence continued to play a large role in the post-medieval world, and he is considered by many as the father of research and empirical science, and the founder of such diverse disciplines as logic, psychology, political science, literary criticism, scientific grammar, physics, physiology, biology and most other natural sciences.

Some scholars, in fact, have described the intellectual history of western civilization as a permanent debate in which Aristotle has sometimes triumphed and sometimes not, but in which at all times his spirit and principles have acted as the substructure and inspiration of progress.

Critical Essays Dealing With Plato's Philosophy on "The Good Life"

The foundation of Plato's theory on the good life rests on the idea that everything has one function or use which it is naturally suited for. The justness, beauty, virtue and excellence of the particular thing all depends on the fulfillment of that function. According to this idea, even man has one function for which he is naturally suited. Man is, of course, a bit more complicated than a chair or a horse, so figuring out his proper function is by no means an easy task and one subject to much debate. For Plato, though, man's function is dictated by nature and thus objective.

There is no relativism or subjectivism involved; each man cannot decide for himself what his function is. Rather, there is one universal function dictated by nature that is the same for all people in all circumstances and situations.

In the Republic Plato argues that the proper uses or function of man and his soul is to live justly and to achieve a state of unity and harmony. Man consists of several parts, each different and with different aims, goals and appetites. He lists the intellect, spirit/courage, and physical desires as the three parts of the soul, though he may simplify this for ease of understanding. That's irrelevant though, it's just important to conceptualize the soul as composed of several conflicting parts. But this state of conflict is undesirable and man must attempt to harmonize his soul. This can be done by teaching each part to perform its function as nature dictates, without interfering in the business of other parts. It is important to realise that each part is intended to perform its role well, not just to perform it. So, in the case of physical desires, pursuing all types of luxurious pleasures is not a job well done; that part of the soul should simply aim at survival and good health. When all of these parts are pursuing their aims in an appropriate fashion, there can still be some conflicts. It is the job of reason in circumstances such as these to intervene with other aims, intent on balancing the soul, providing some satisfaction for all. When this is accomplished, when the parts of the soul are fulfilling their natural functions well and, under the guidance of reason, are in harmony and balance with the others, then the soul is just, unified, good and happy.

But for Plato this does not seem to be quite enough. This is an appropriate and fitting state of being, but surely just being is not performing one's natural function. A knife may be sharp, smooth, clean, well-balanced and of good size, but until it starts cutting it is not performing its function. And so the above description is not man's function, but merely the state of affairs or being required to properly perform his function. It is in the Phaedo and Apology that we get a sense of man's proper, natural function. He is to pursue knowledge, intelligence, and ultimate reality. This is the way man truly attains virtue and it is on par with the path of the gods. In The Republic Plato argues similarly, proposing that man is to search for the good and the other forms. In both these cases man's function is to use his mind/intellect/ reason in search of truth, knowledge and ultimate reality. The body is a hindrance, an obstacle in this search and it must be struggled against by the soul at all times. It plagues the mind with all sorts of desires and appetites, barely giving the mind time to think. So it is the job of man to remove himself as entirely as he can from his body, to use it only in the barest, simplest fashion, only to survive. In this way he will minimize its impediment and allow himself to pursue his true function to the maximum of his ability. And this quest and search is man's function and the only way to the good life. It depends on the justice and harmonization of the soul. Socrates even admits in The Republic that he himself knows not just what the good is, but he knows we should strive for it and the knowledge of it.

All of this is fine and good, a noble pursuit, but it seems like just another attempt to create meaning and give structure to our lives. The pursuit of knowledge is admirable and I think very worthy, but in terms of inherent value or meaning, I think it is the same as watching game shows all day or dedicating your life to sport or vice. One is, ultimately, just as good as the next and gets you just as far. You just need to decide what is important in your life and what you want to do with it. In addition, I think it is a mistake to place so much value on the mind/intellect. Any talk of ultimate reality and absolute truth seems overblown and arrogant. Our minds are limited, weak, fallible instruments, just as our senses are. They too, can mislead and misguide us, and I see no reason to suppose they are powerful enough to solve the riddle of the universe. For that matter, I see no reason to believe there even is a riddle to be solved. Perhaps we just developed a survival tool that, now that our survival is secure, is trying to occupy itself and keep itself busy, all for nothing. If this is accurate, then one philosophy is just as good as the next, depending solely on personal tastes.

Bibliography

- *Ackrill J. L.* 2001. Essays on Plato and Aristotle, USA
- *Adler, Mortimer J.* (1978). Aristotle for Everybody. New York: Macmillan. A popular exposition for the general reader.
- Bakalis Nikolaos. 2005. *Handbook of Greek Philosophy:* From Thales to the Stoics Analysis and Fragments, Trafford Publishing ISBN 1-4120-4843-5
- *Barnes J.* 1995. The Cambridge Companion to Aristotle, Cambridge University Press
- *Boche?ski, I. M.* (1951). Ancient Formal Logic. Amsterdam: North-Holland Publishing Company.
- *Bolotin, David* (1998). An Approach to Aristotle's Physics: With Particular Attention to the Role of His Manner of Writing. Albany: SUNY Press. A contribution to our understanding of how to read Aristotle's scientific works.
- *Burnyeat, M. F. et al.* 1979. Notes on Book Zeta of Aristotle's Metaphysics: Sub-faculty of Philosophy
- *Chappell, V.* 1973. Aristotle's Conception of Matter, Journal of Philosophy 70: 679-696
- *Code, Alan.* 1995. Potentiality in Aristotle's Science and Metaphysics, Pacific Philosophical Quarterly 76
- *Frede, Michael.* 1987. Essays in Ancient Philosophy. Minneapolis: University of Minnesota Press
- *Gill, Mary Louise.* 1989. Aristotle on Substance: The Paradox of Unity. Princeton: Princeton University Press

- *Guthrie, W. K. C.* (1981). A History of Greek Philosophy, Vol. 6. Cambridge University Press.
- *Halper, Edward C.* (2007) One and Many in Aris-totle's Metaphysics, Volume 1: Books Alpha-Delta, Parmenides Publishing, ISBN 978-1-930972-21-6
- *Halper, Edward C.* (2005) One and Many in Aristotle's Metaphysics, Volume 2: The Central Books, Parmenides Publishing, ISBN 978-1-930972-05-6
- *Irwin, T. H.* 1988. Aristotle's First Principles. Oxford: Clarendon Press
- Jori, Alberto. 2003. Aristotele, Milano: Bruno Mondadori Editore (Prize 2003 of the *"International Academy of the History of Science"*) ISBN 88-424-9737-1
- *Knight, Kelvin.* 2007. Aristotelian Philosophy: Ethics and Politics from Aristotle to MacIntyre, Polity Press.
- *Lewis, Frank A.* 1991. Substance and Predication in Aristotle. Cambridge: Cambridge University Press.
- *Lloyd, G. E. R.* 1968. Aristotle: The Growth and Structure of his Thought. Cambridge: Cambridge Univ. Pr., ISBN 0-521-09456-9.
- *Lord, Carnes.* 1984. Introduction to The Politics, by Aristotle. Chicago: Chicago University Press.
- *Loux, Michael J.* 1991. Primary Ousia: An Essay on Aristotle's Metaphysics. Ithaca, NY: Cornell University Press
- *Owen, G. E. L.* 1965c. The Platonism of Aristotle, Proceedings of the British Academy 50 125-150. Reprinted in J. Barnes, M. Schofield, and R. R. K. Sorabji (eds.), Articles on Aristotle, Vol 1. Science. London: Duckworth (1975). 14-34
- *Pangle, Lorraine Smith* (2003). Aristotle and the Philosophy of Friendship. Cambridge: Cambridge University Press. Aristotle's conception of the deepest human relationship viewed in the light of the history of philosophic thought on friendship.
- *Reeve, C. D. C.* 2000. Substantial Knowledge: Aristotle's Metaphysics. Indianapolis: Hackett.

- *Rose, Lynn E.* (1968). Aristotle's Syllogistic. Springfield: Charles C Thomas Publisher.
- *Ross, Sir David* (1995). Aristotle, 6th ed., London: Routledge. An classic overview by one of Aristotle's most prominent English translators, in print since 1923.
- *Scaltsas, T.* 1994. Substances and Universals in Aristotle's Metaphysics. Ithaca: Cornell University Press.
- Strauss, Leo. "*On Aristotle's Politics*" (1964), in The City and Man, Chicago; Rand McNally.
- Taylor, Henry Osborn (1922). "*Chapter 3: Aristotle's Biology*", Greek Biology and Medicine.
- Veatch, Henry B. (1974). Aristotle: A Contemporary Appreciation. Bloomington: Indiana U. Press. For the general reader.
- Woods, M. J. 1991b. "*Universals and Particular Forms in Aristotle's Metaphysics.*" Oxford Studies in Ancient Philosophy supplement. 41-56